Rock and Roll Coloring Book

Robert House

Chuck Berry

David Bowie

Sterling Morrison (The Velvet Underground)

The Clash

Ariana Grande

Elvis Presley

Robert Plant

Jimmy Page

Pink Floyd

Stewart Copeland (The Police)

Mick Jagger

Keith Richards

The Sex Pistols

Eric Clapton

Michael Jackson

Jim Morrison

Joan Baez and Bob Dylan

The Ramones

Howlin' Wolf

Kiss

Kurt Cobain (Nirvana)

Kim Gordon (Sonic Youth)

Shane MacGowan (The Pogues)

Freddie Mercury (Queen)

Jonny Greenwood (Radiohead)

Pussy Riot

Marilyn Manson

James Brown

The Rolling Stones

The Beatles

The Carter Family

Gogol Bordello

The Jimi Hendrix Experience

Madonna

The Doors

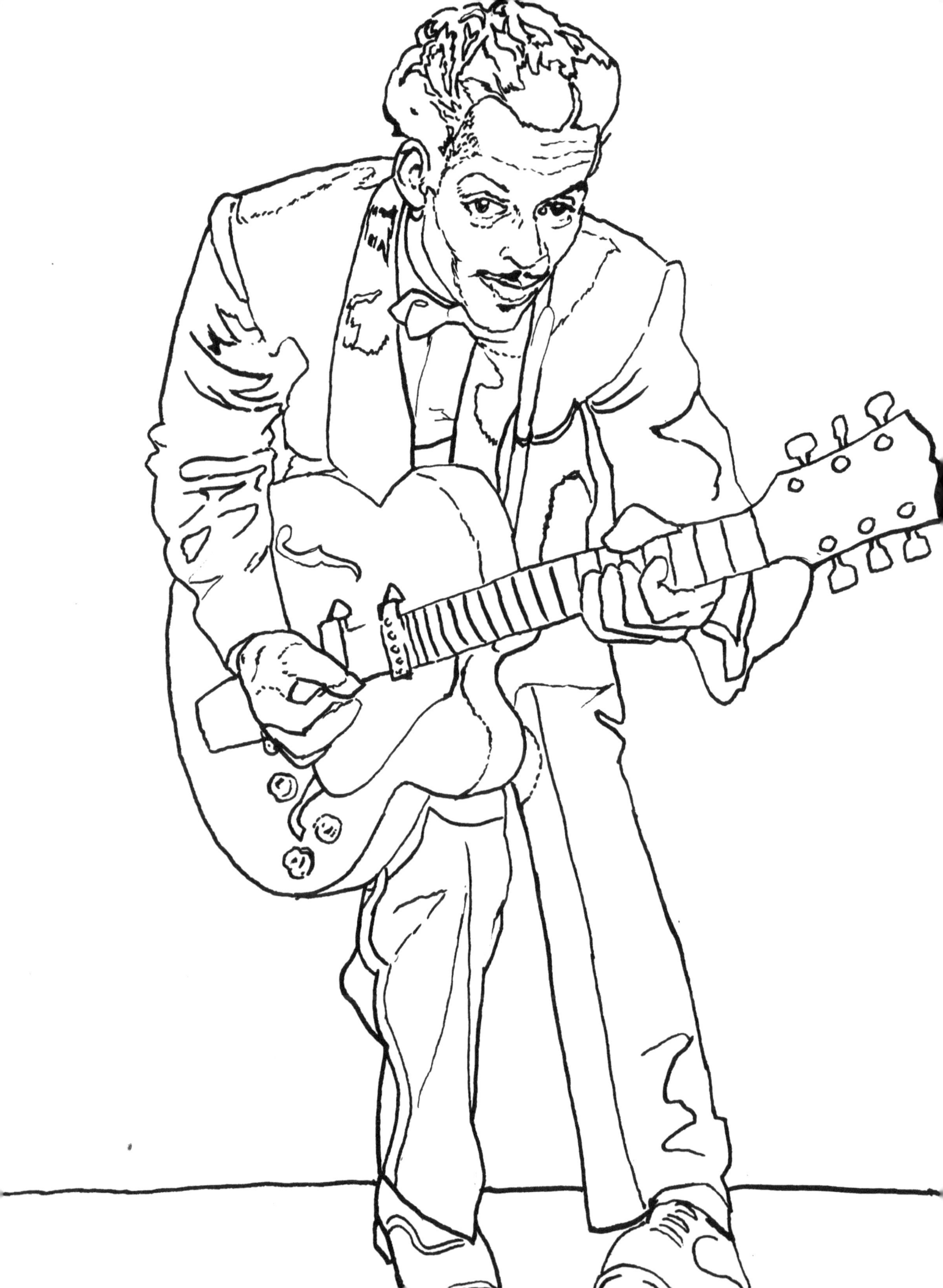

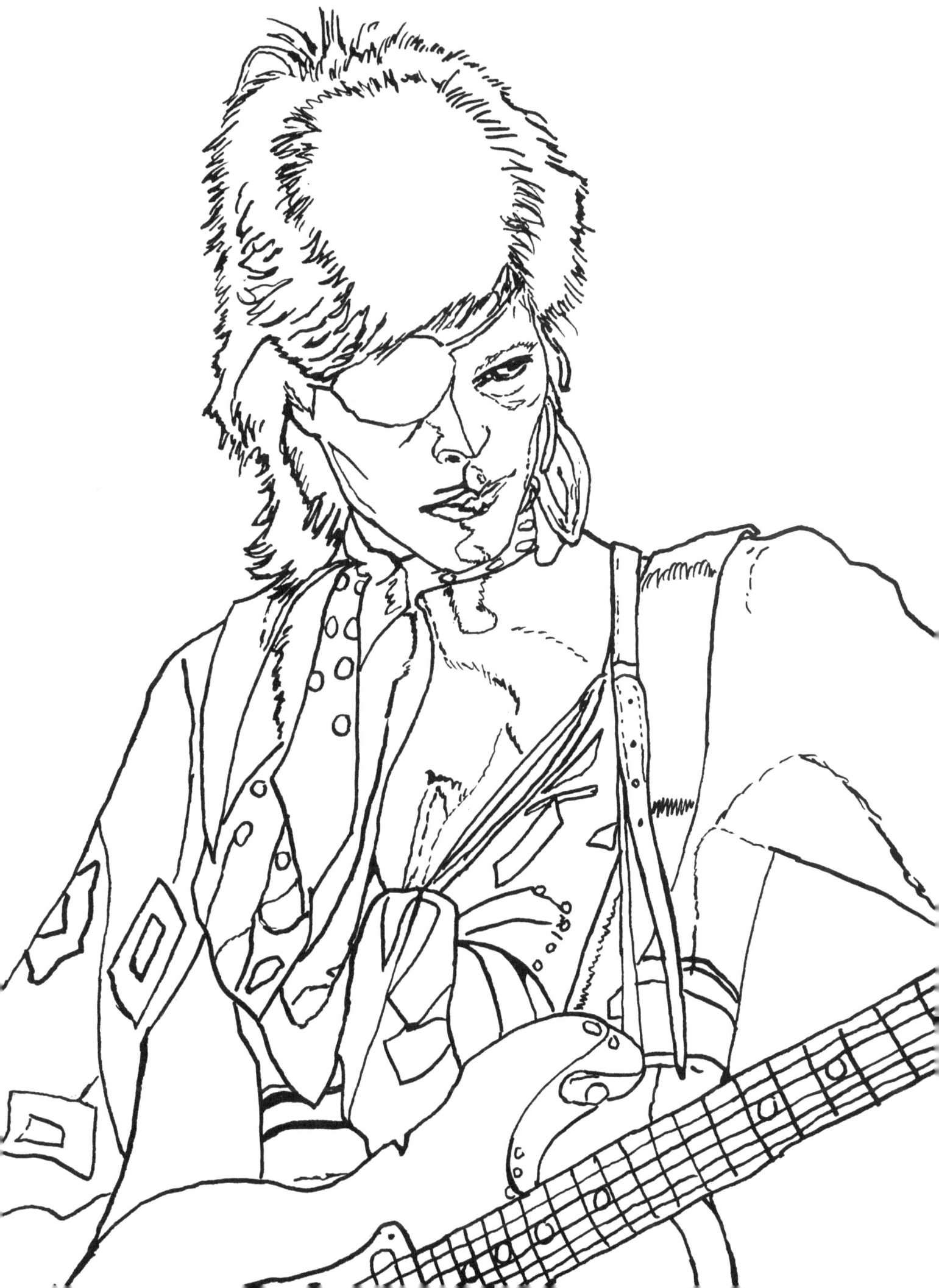

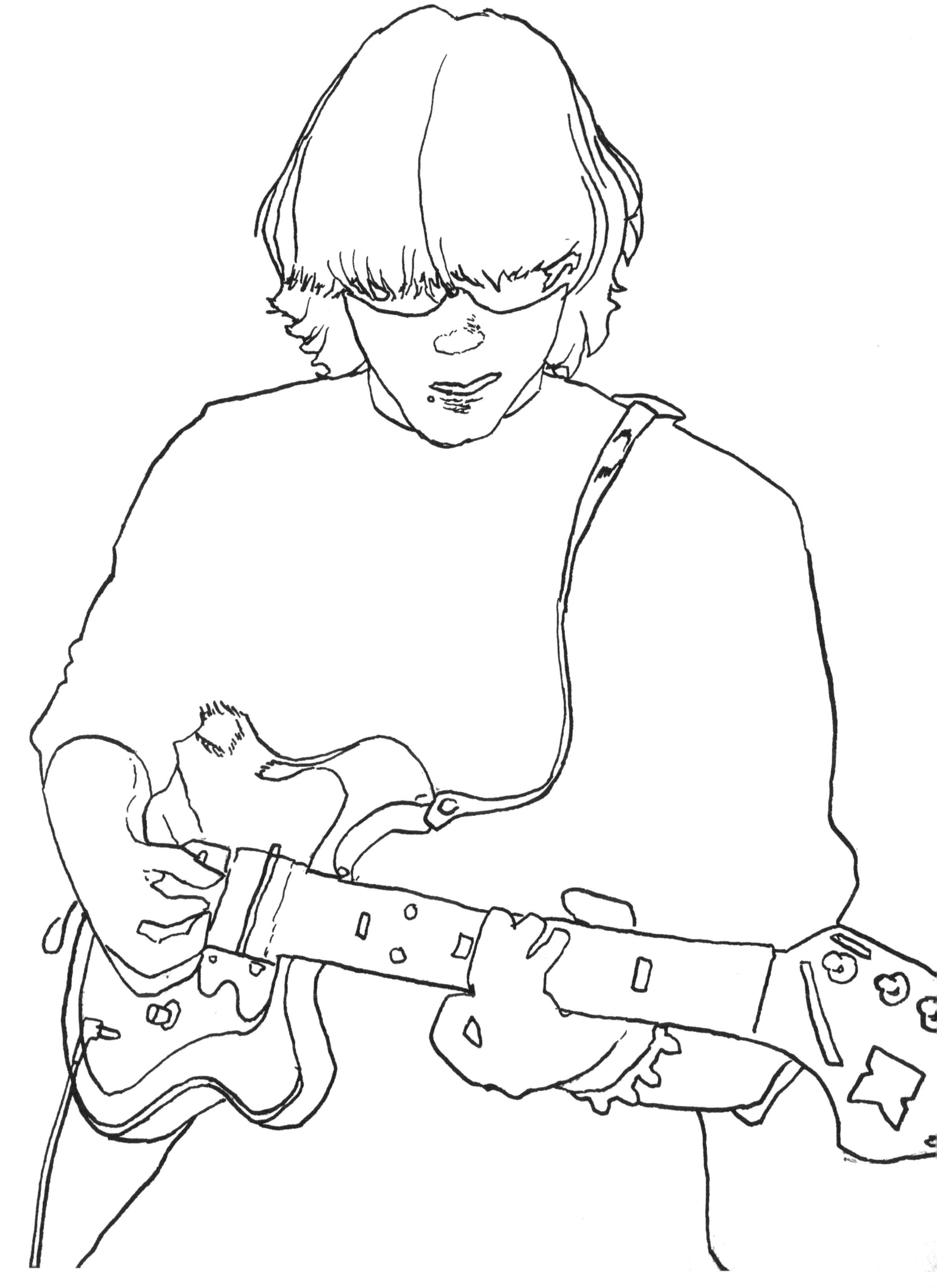

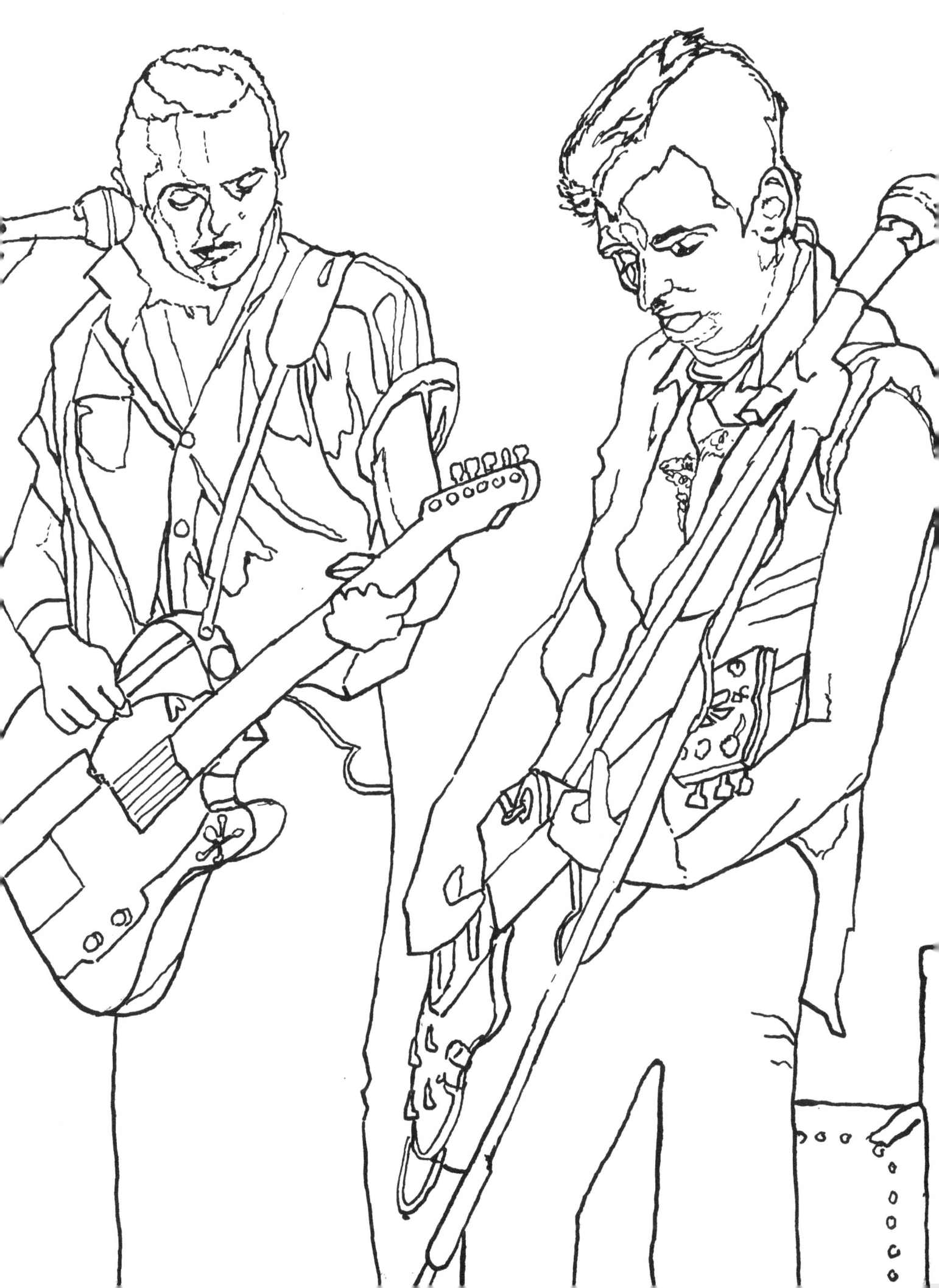

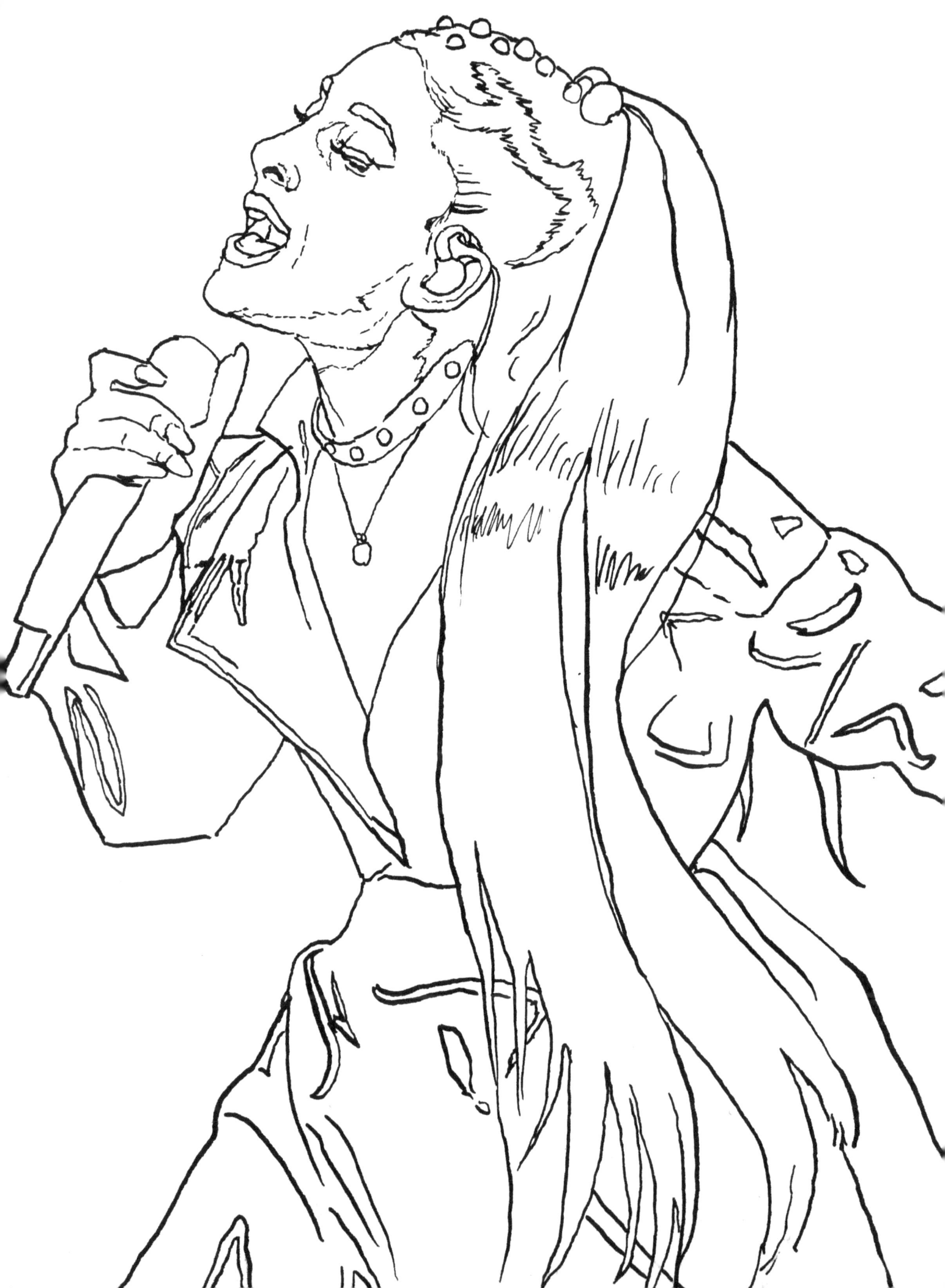

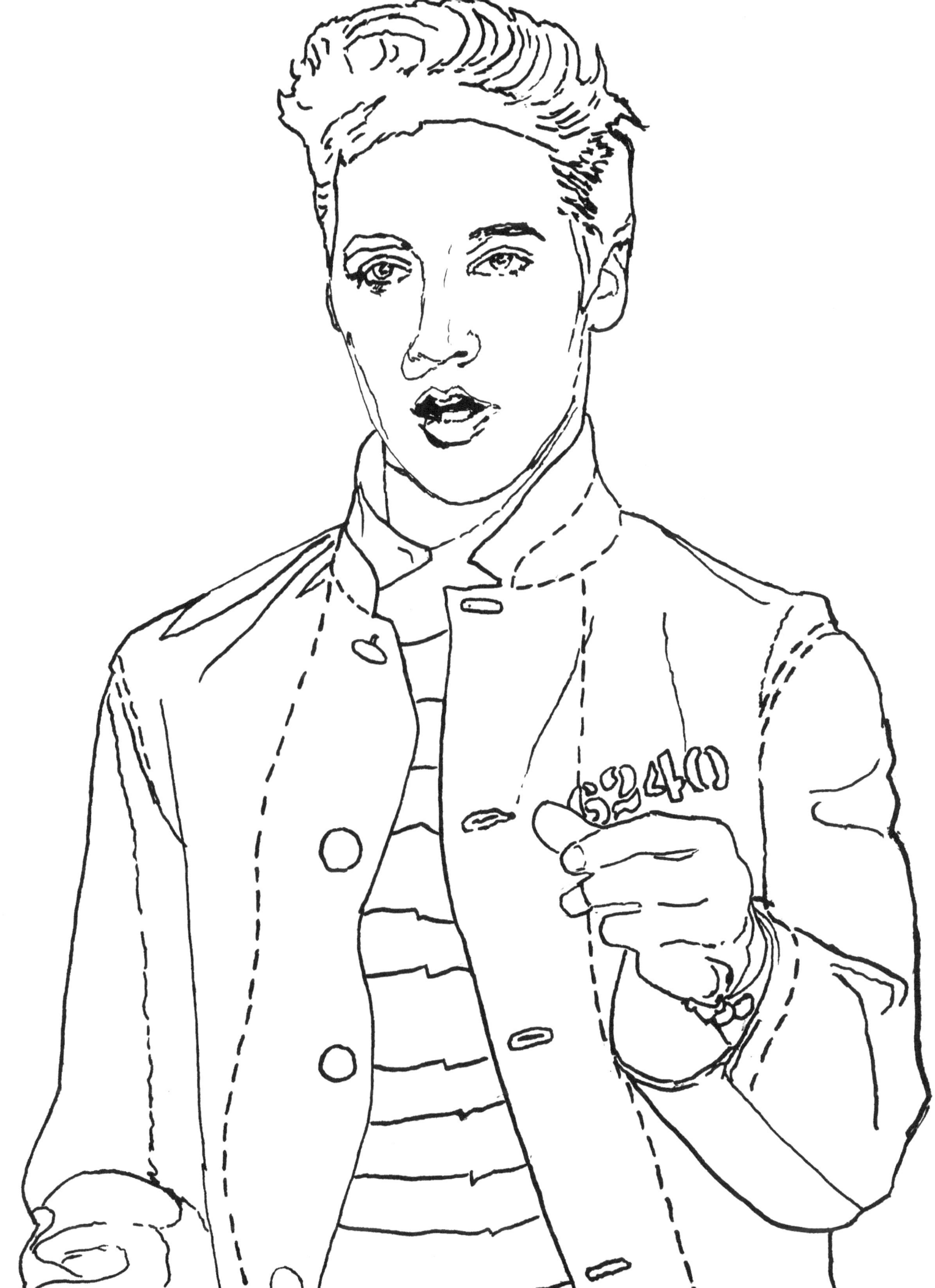

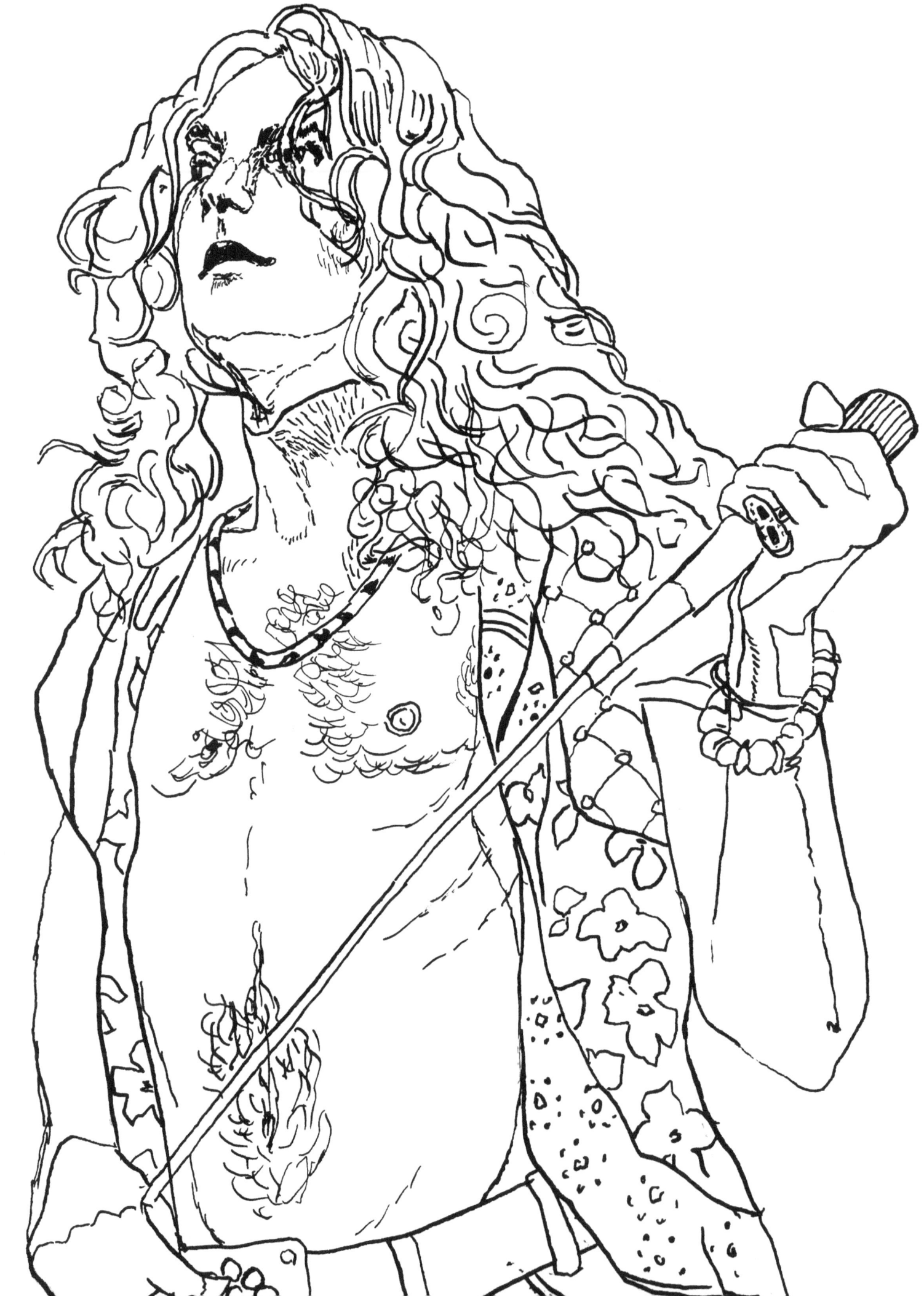

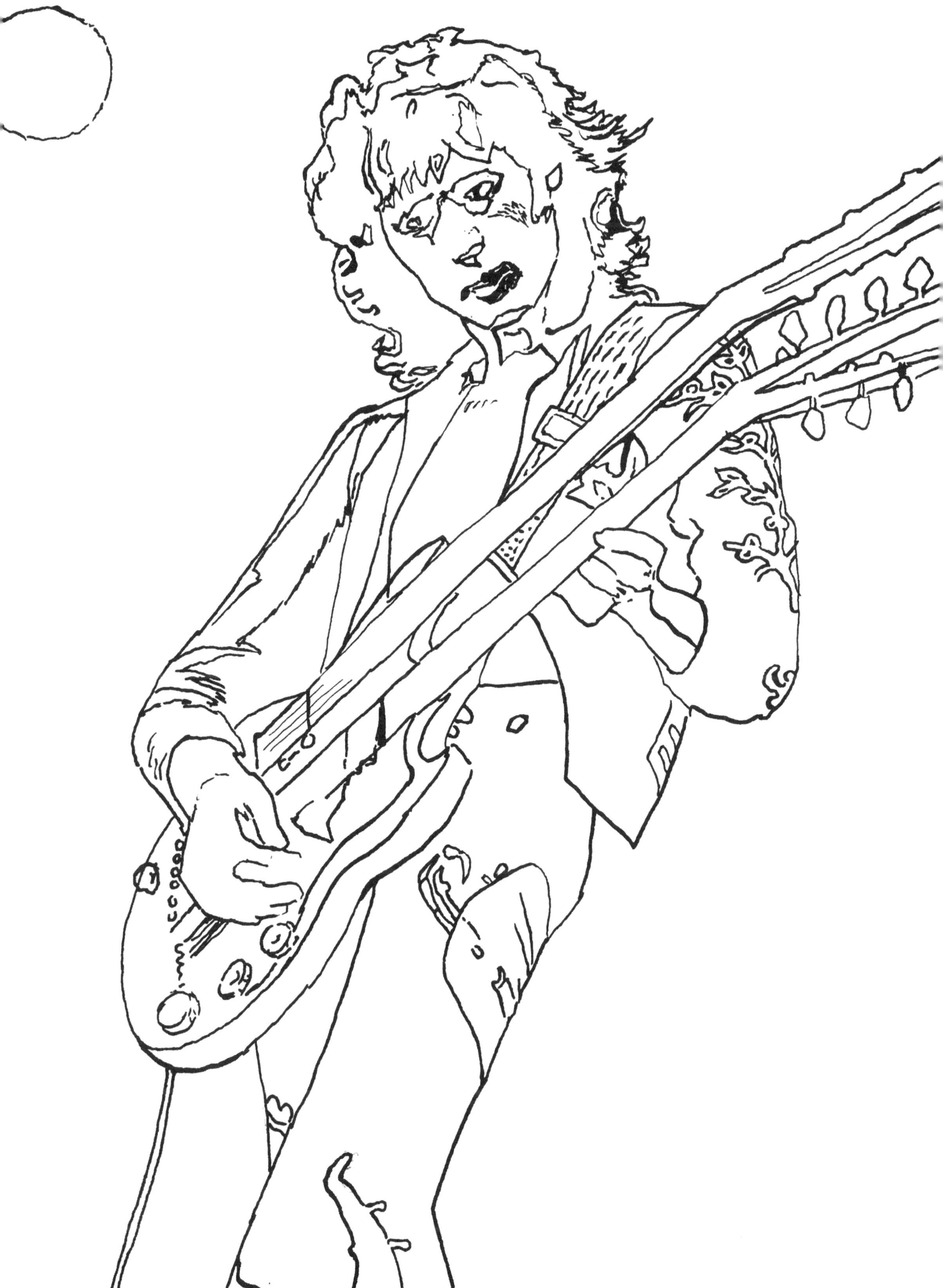

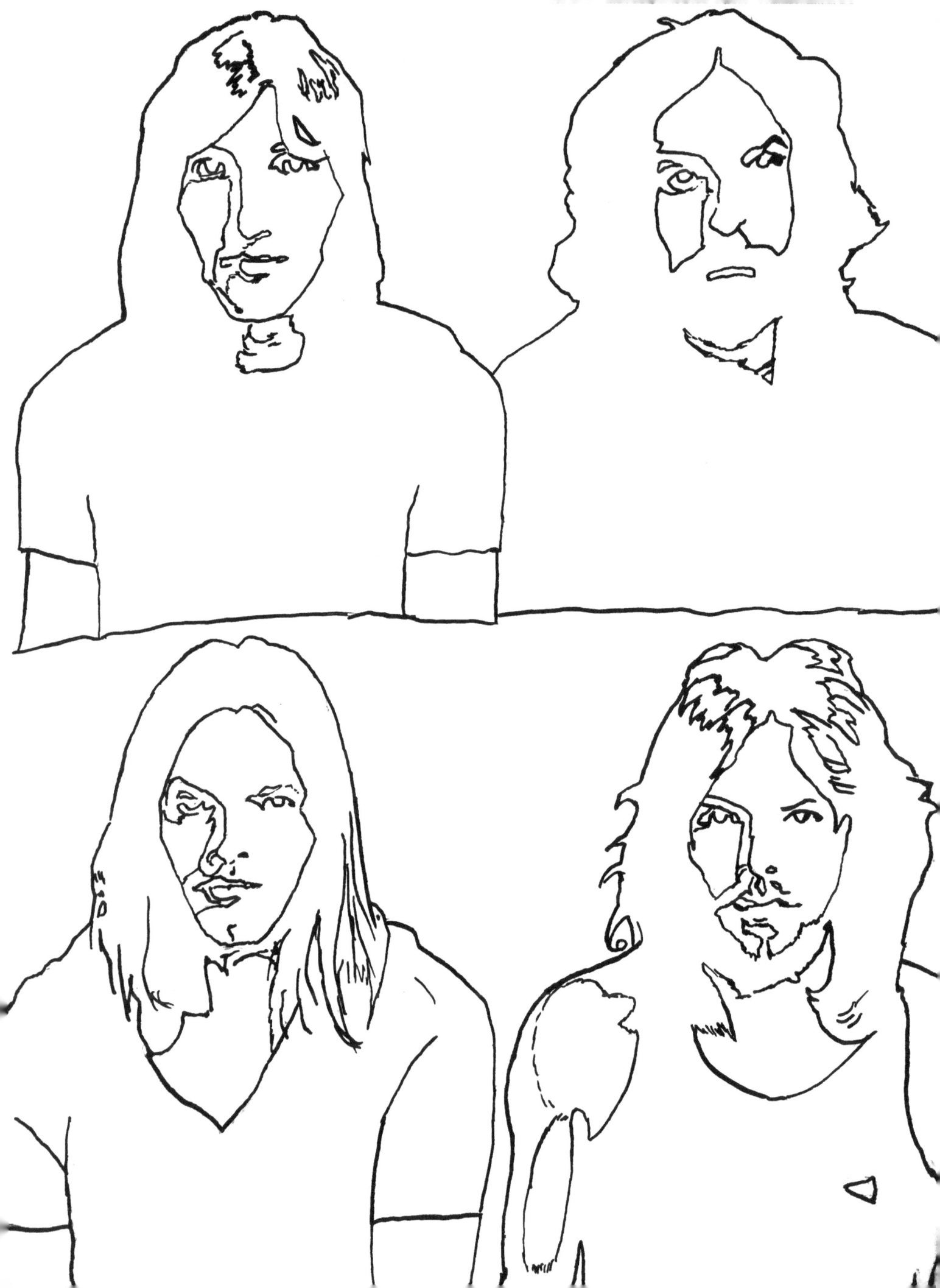

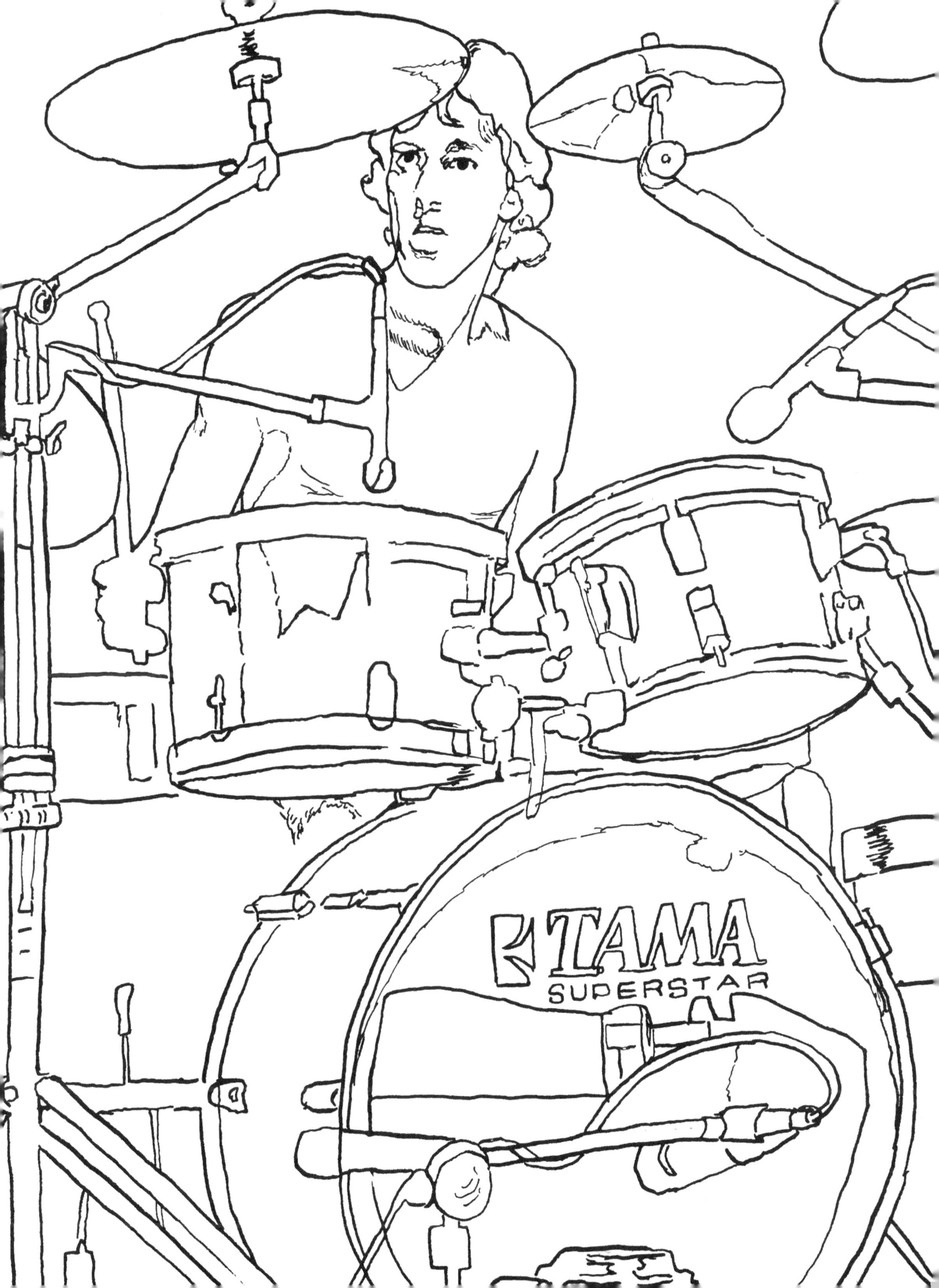

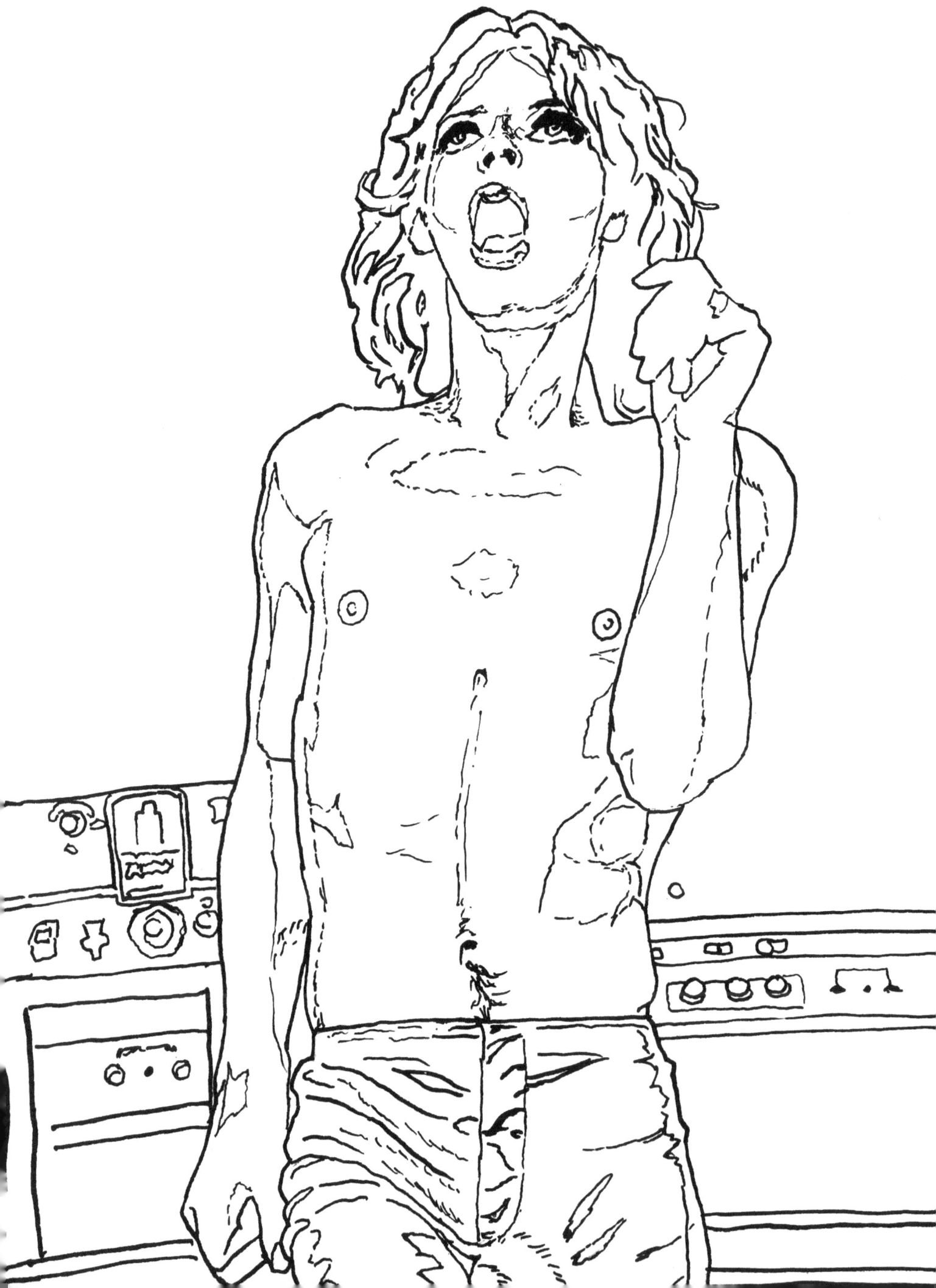

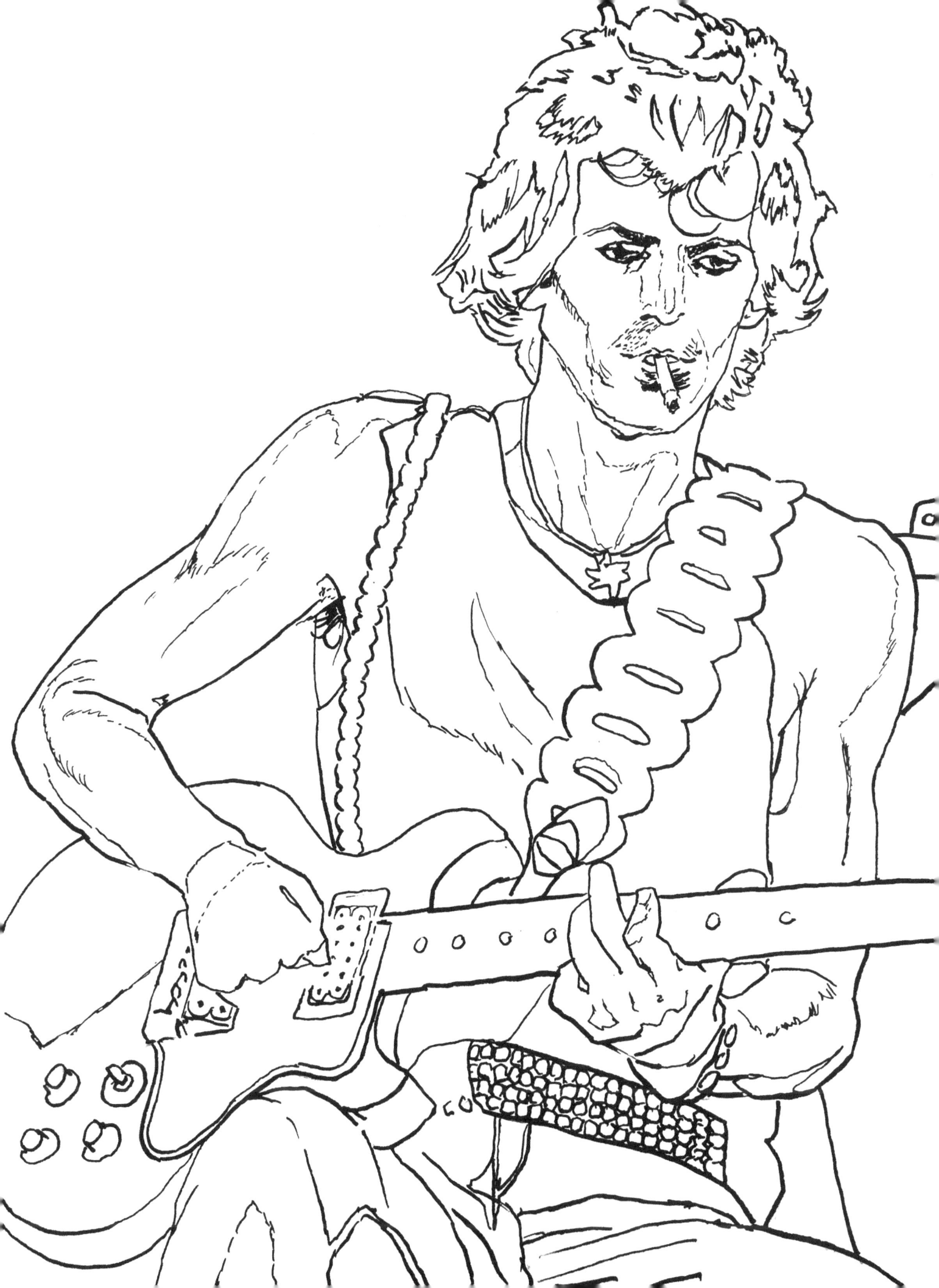

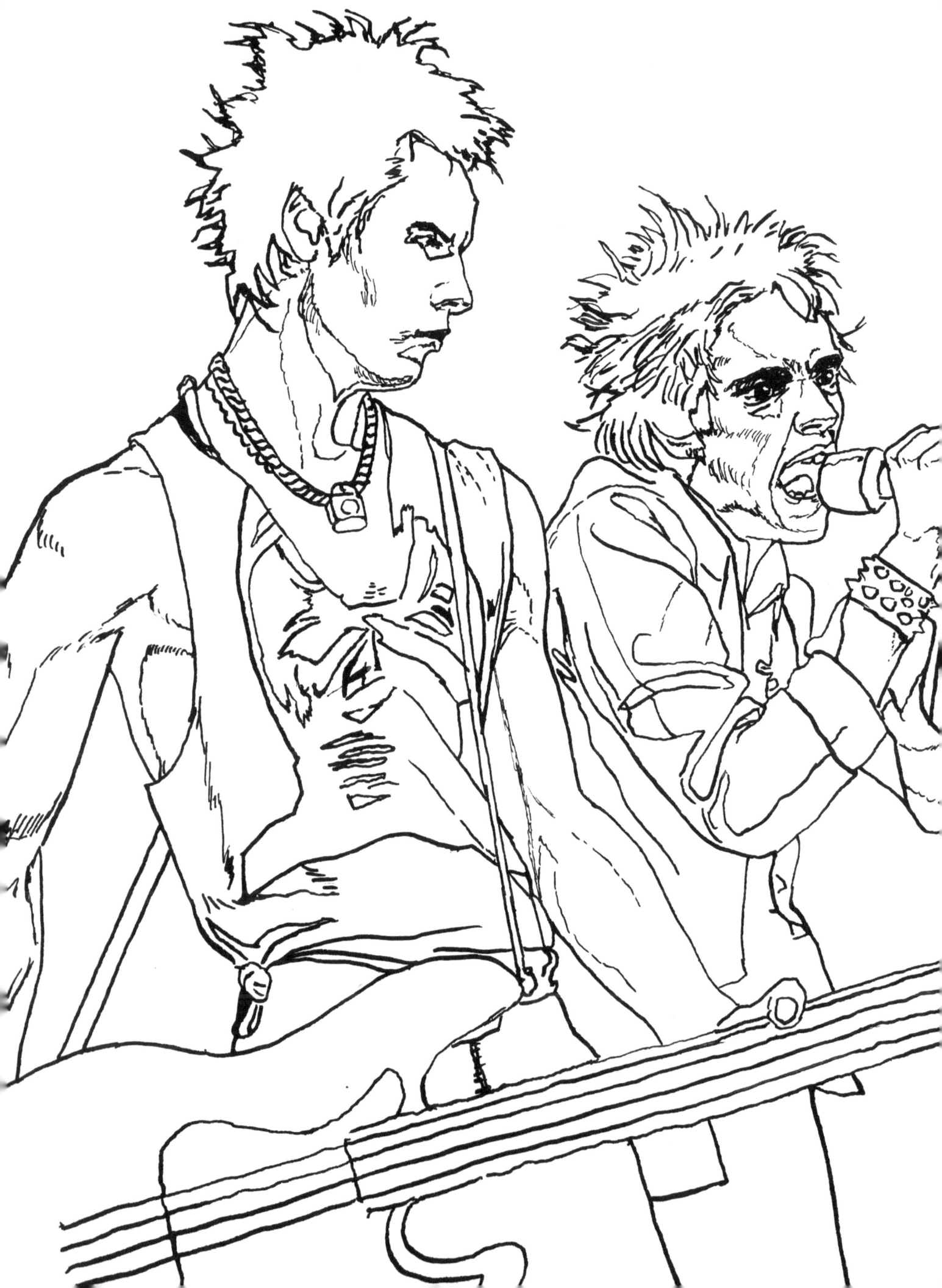

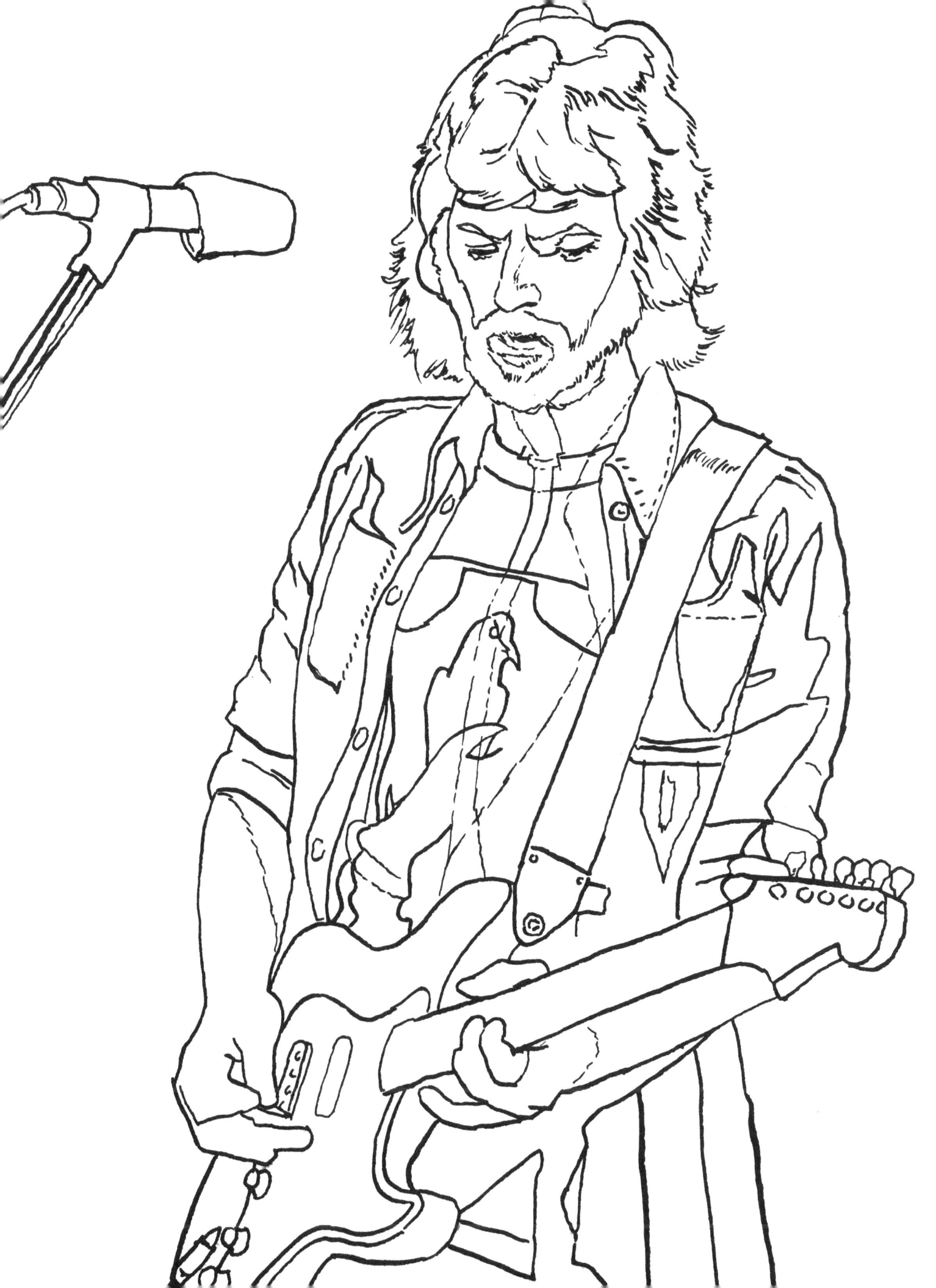

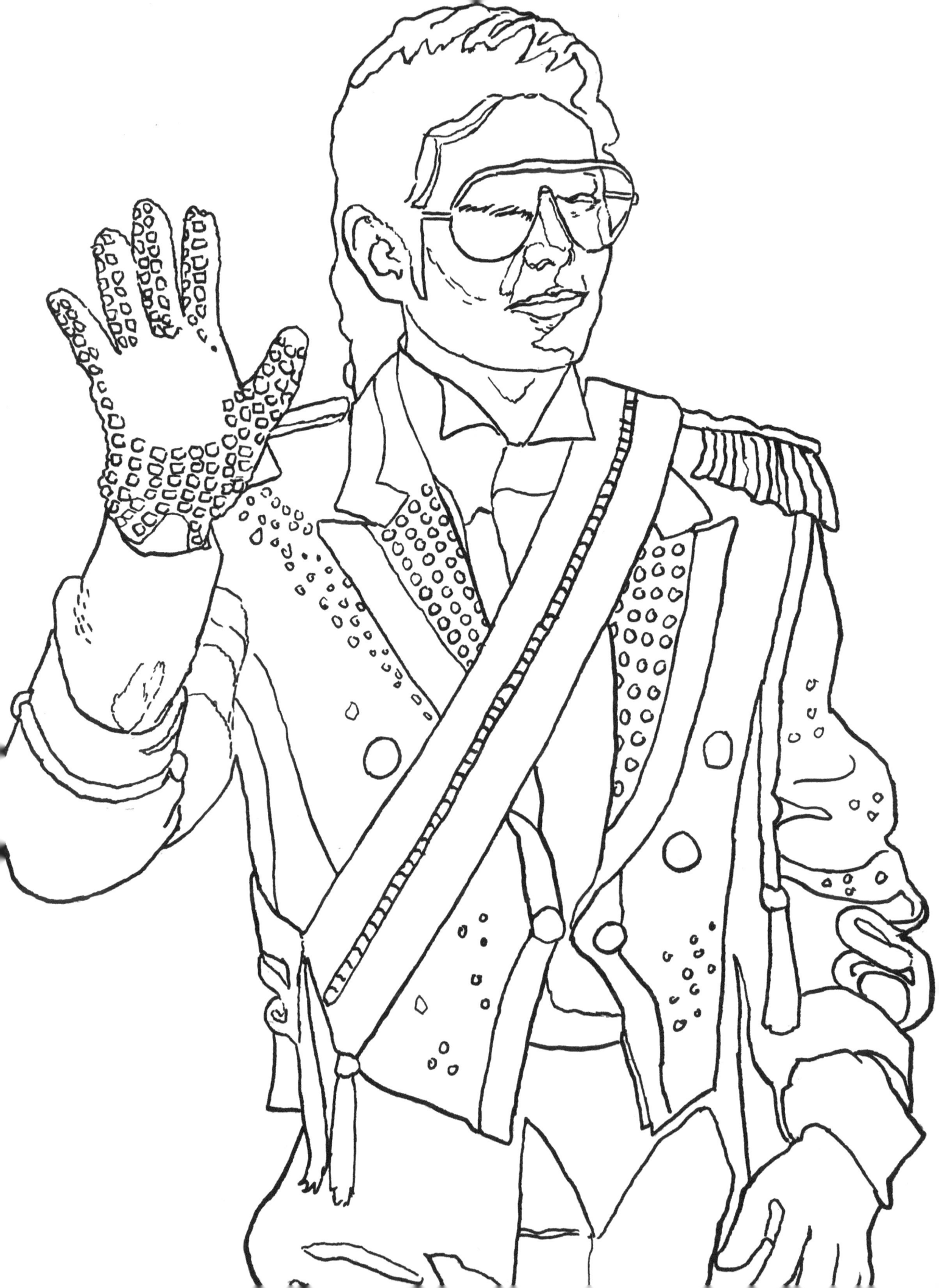

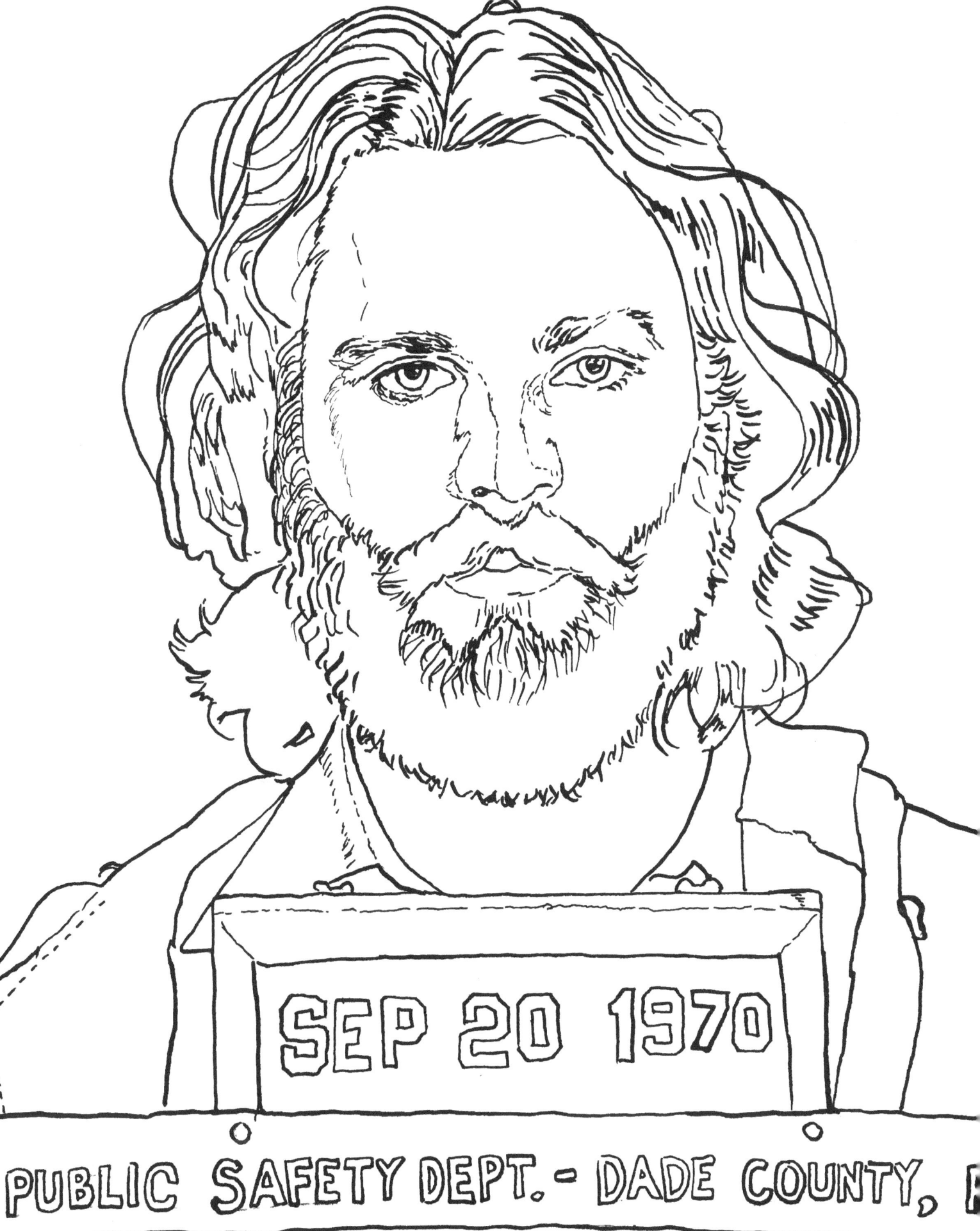

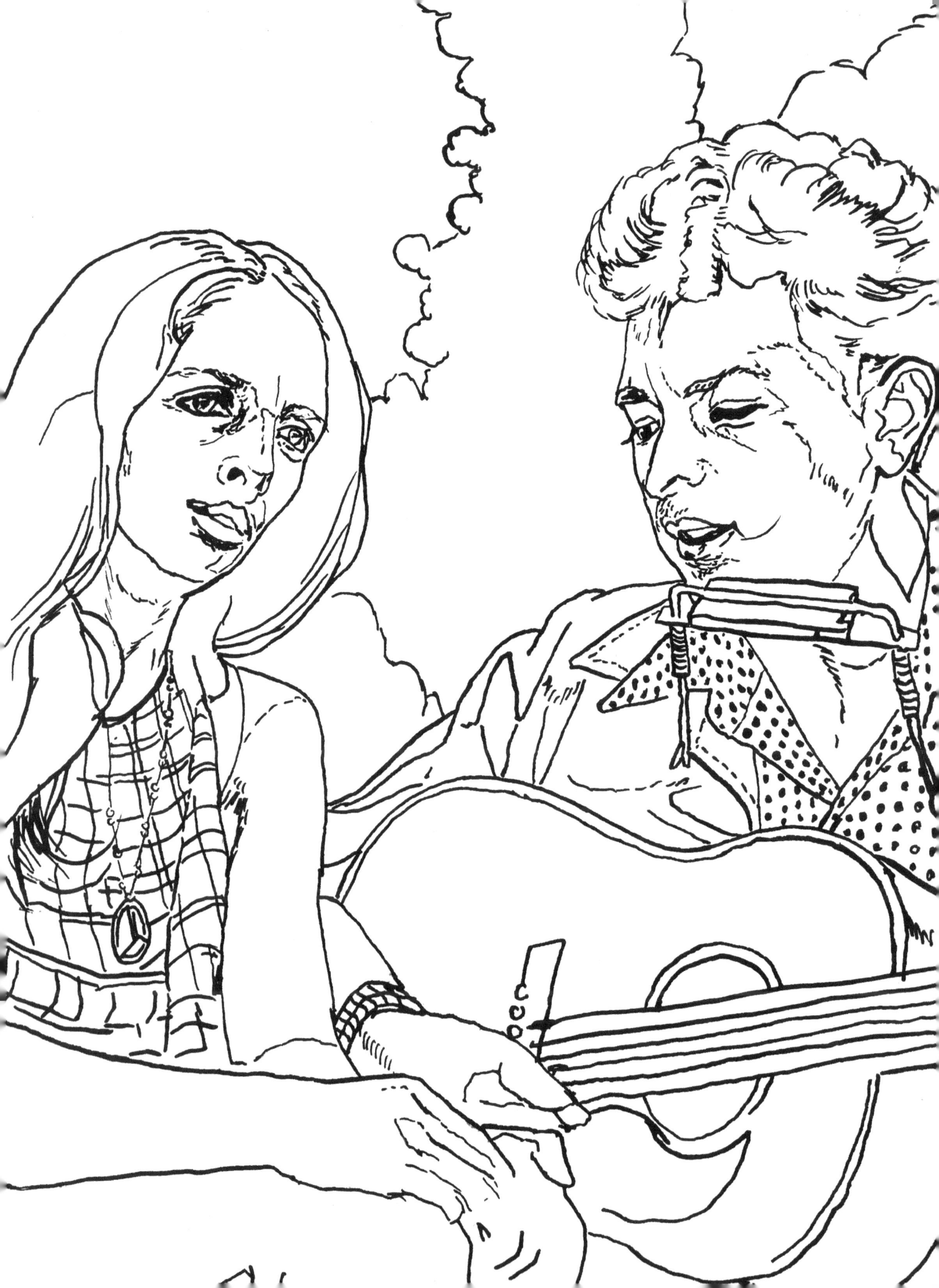

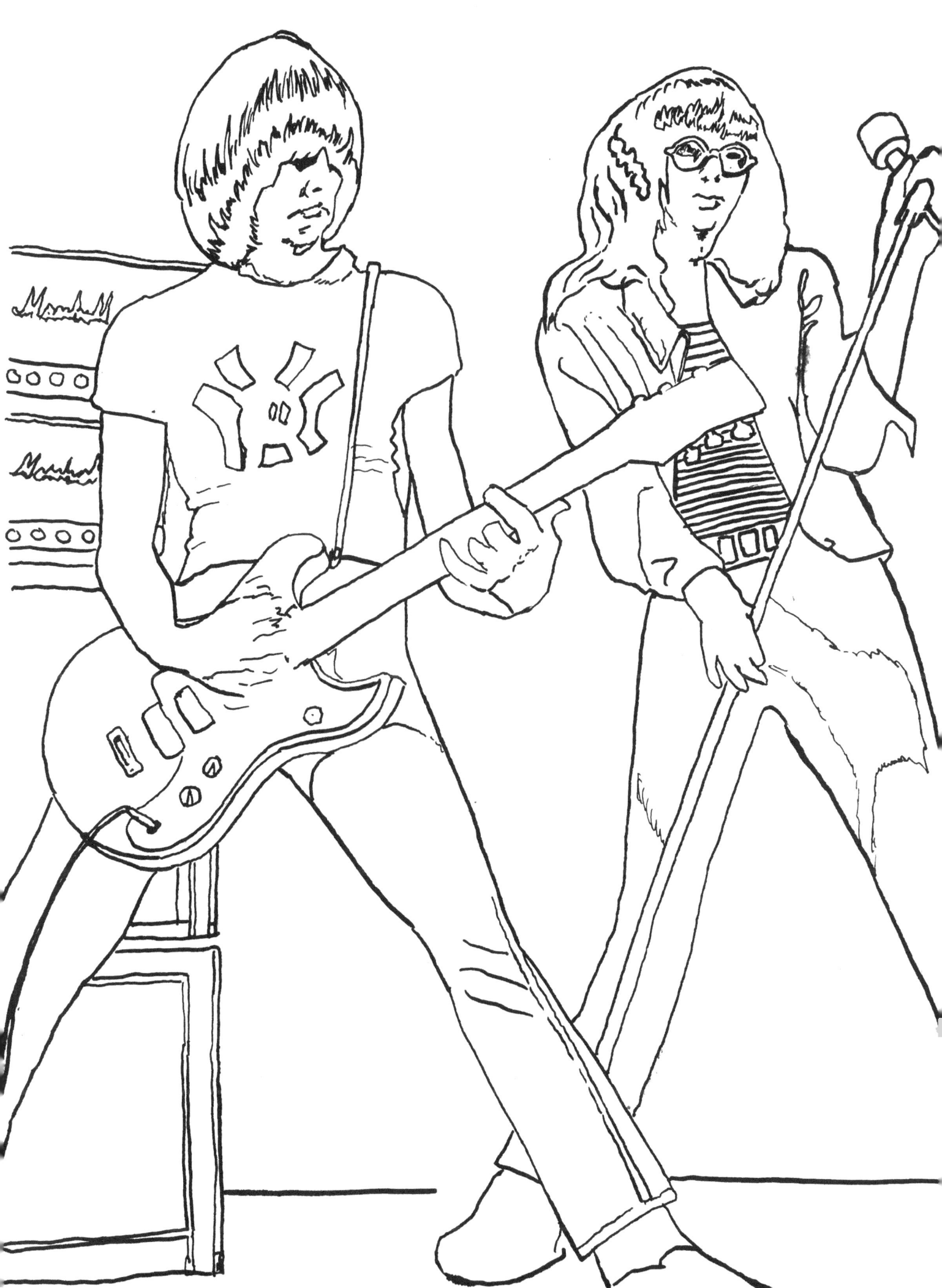

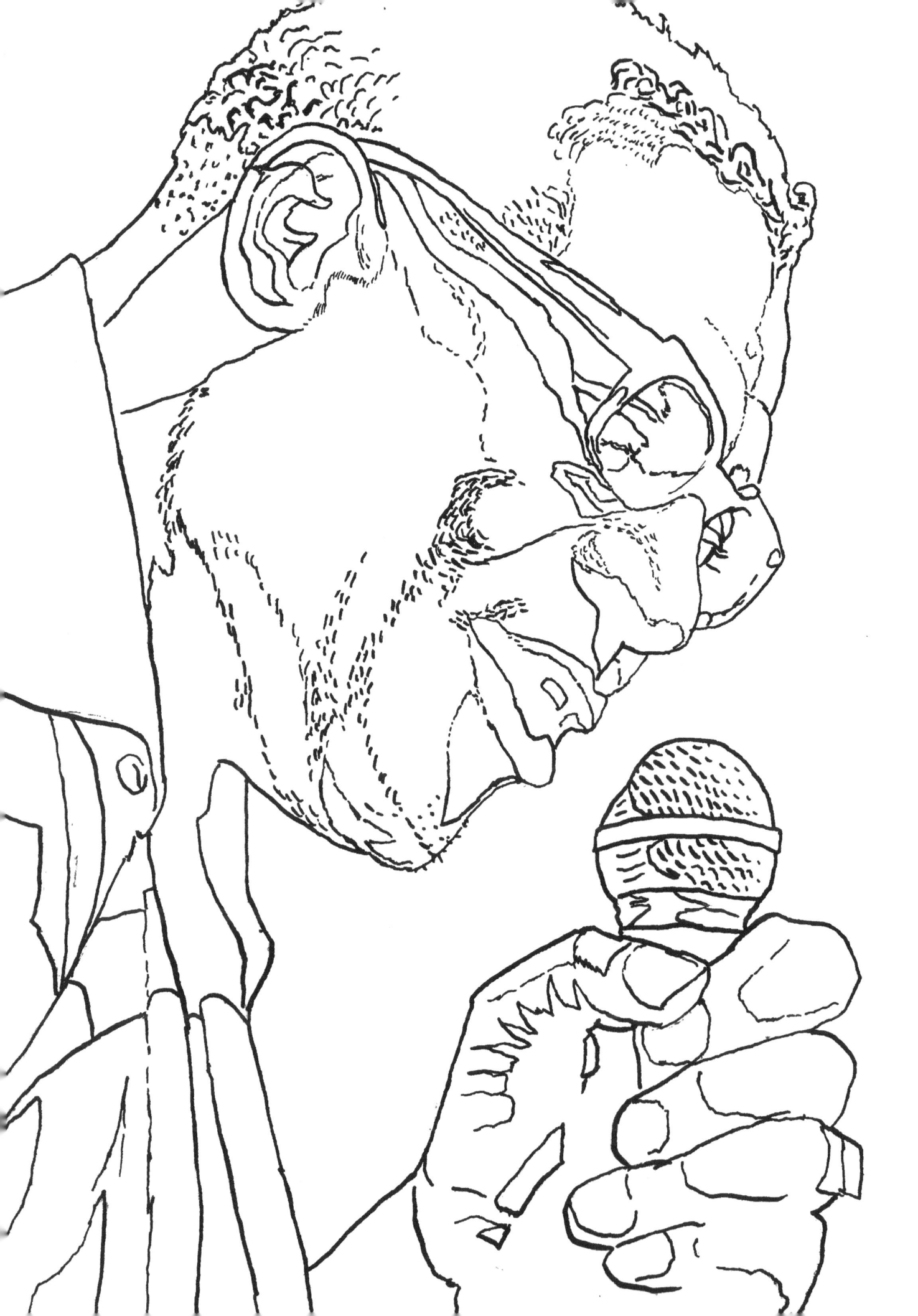

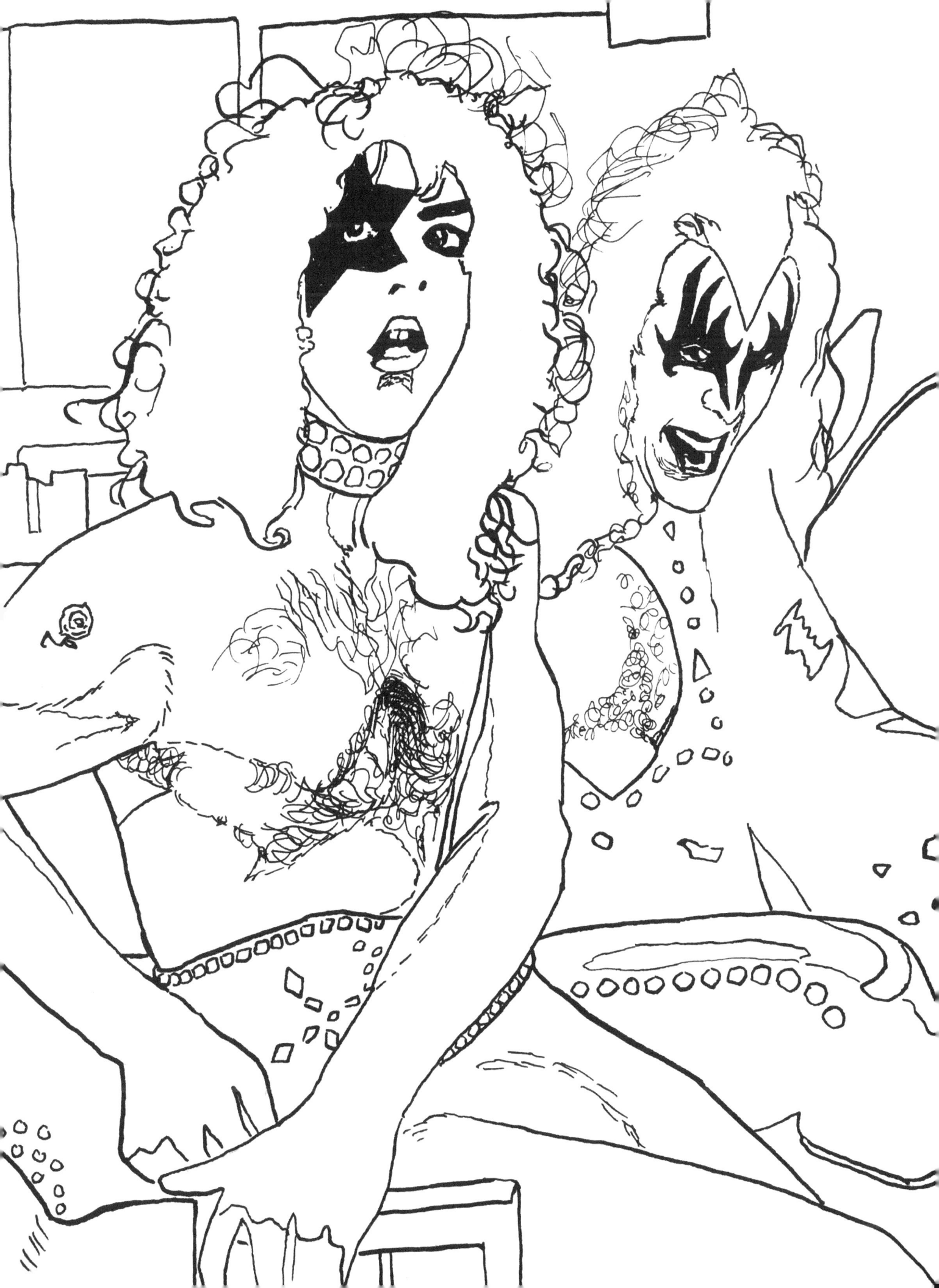

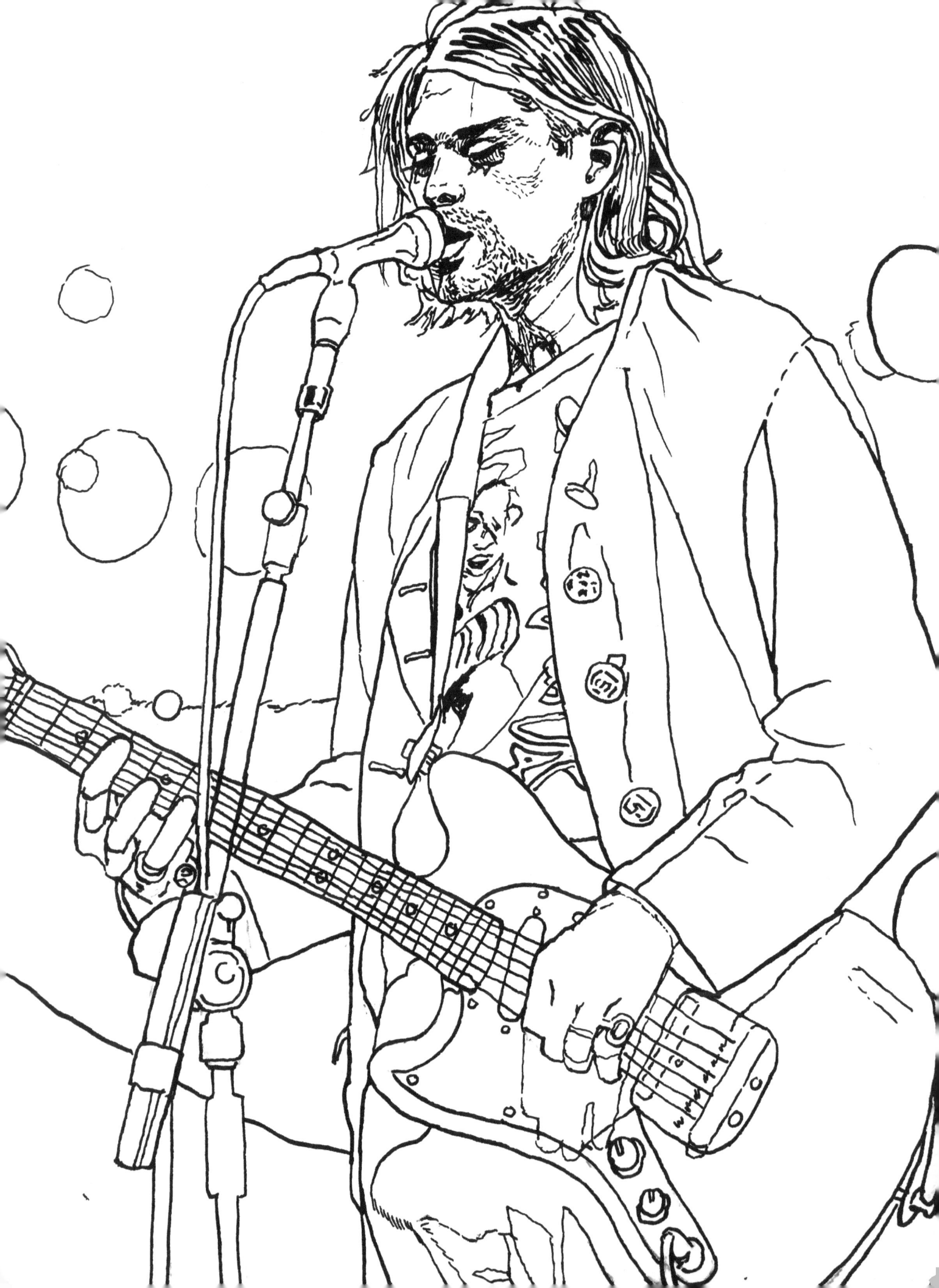

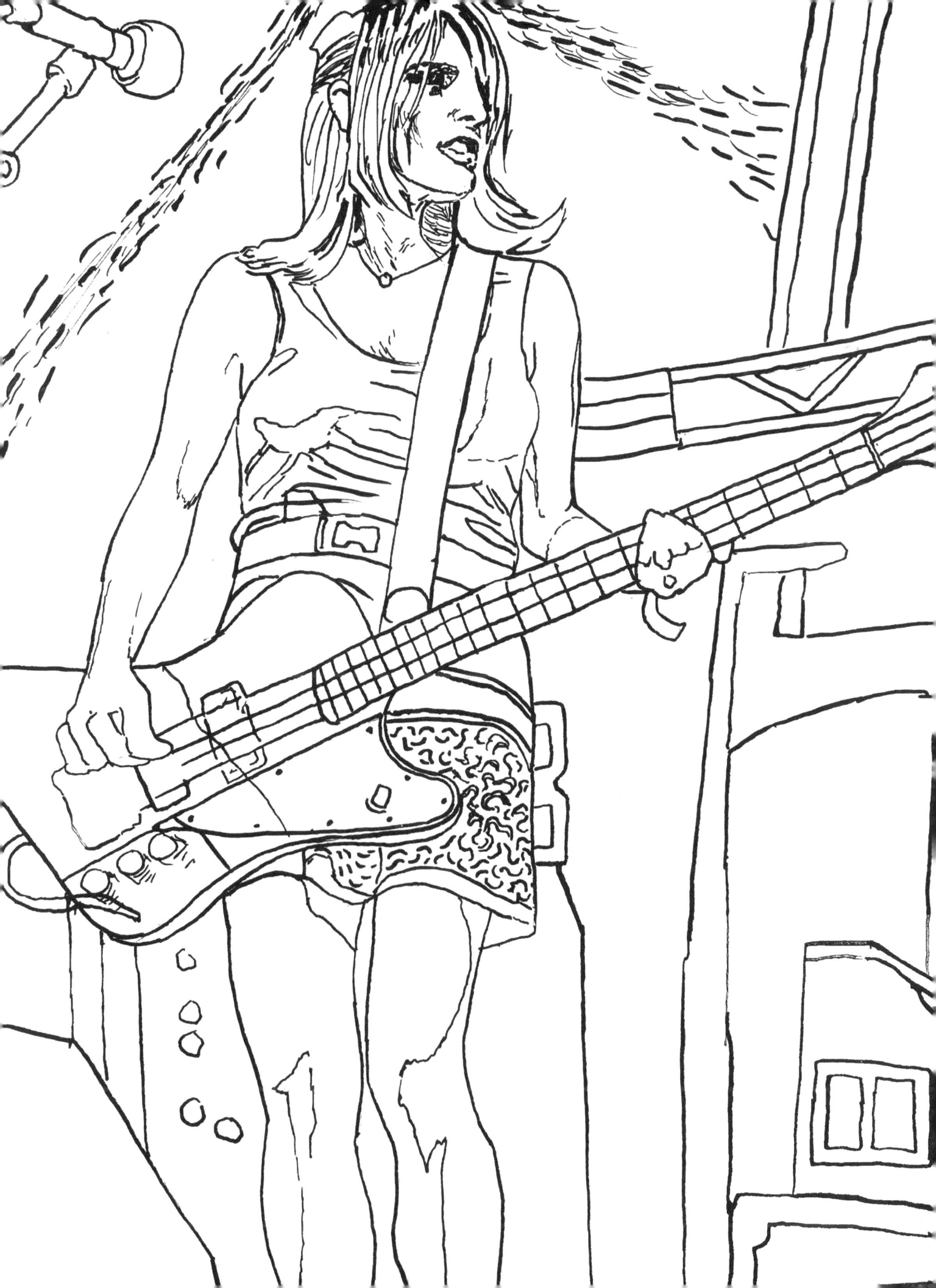

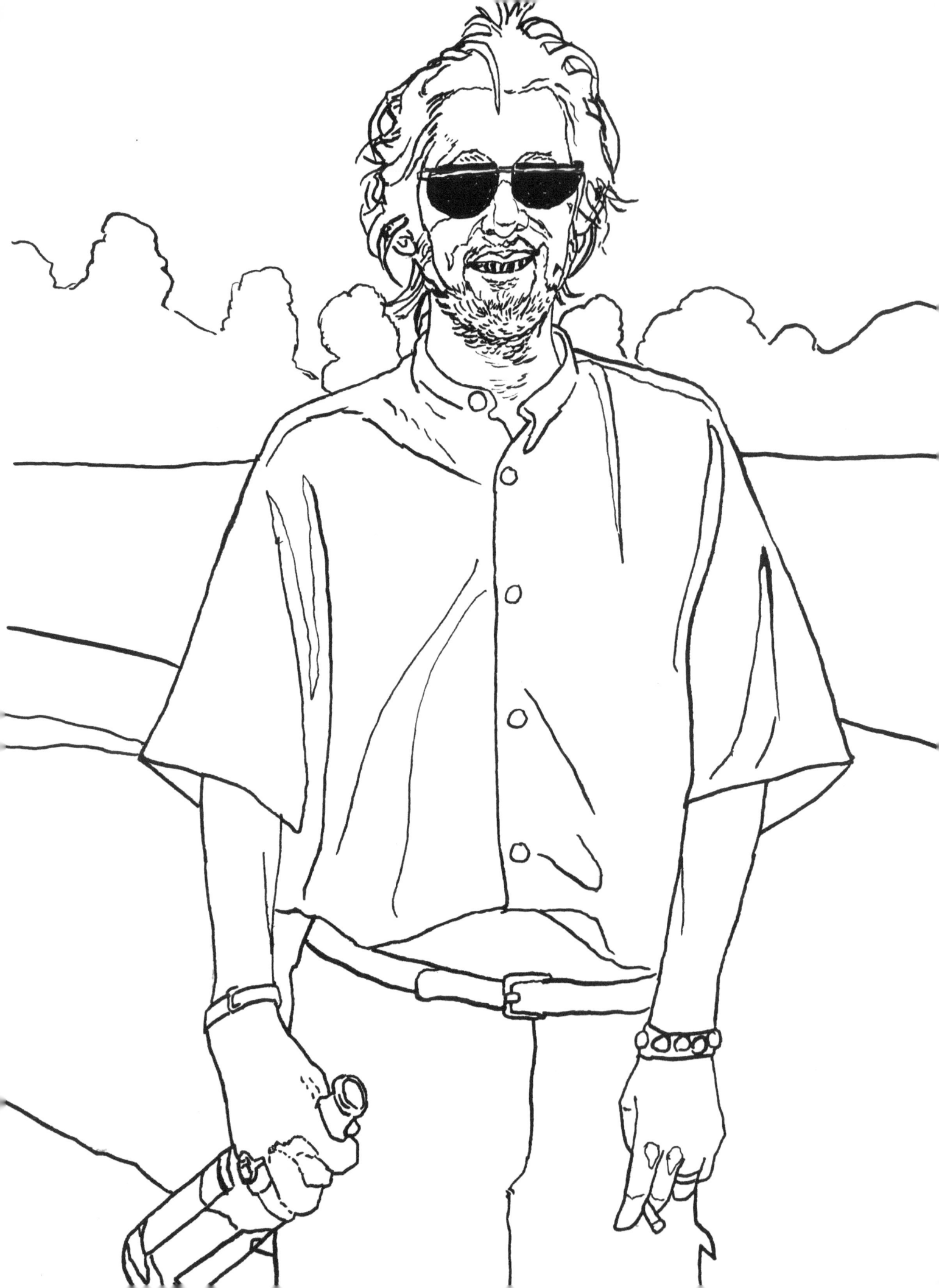

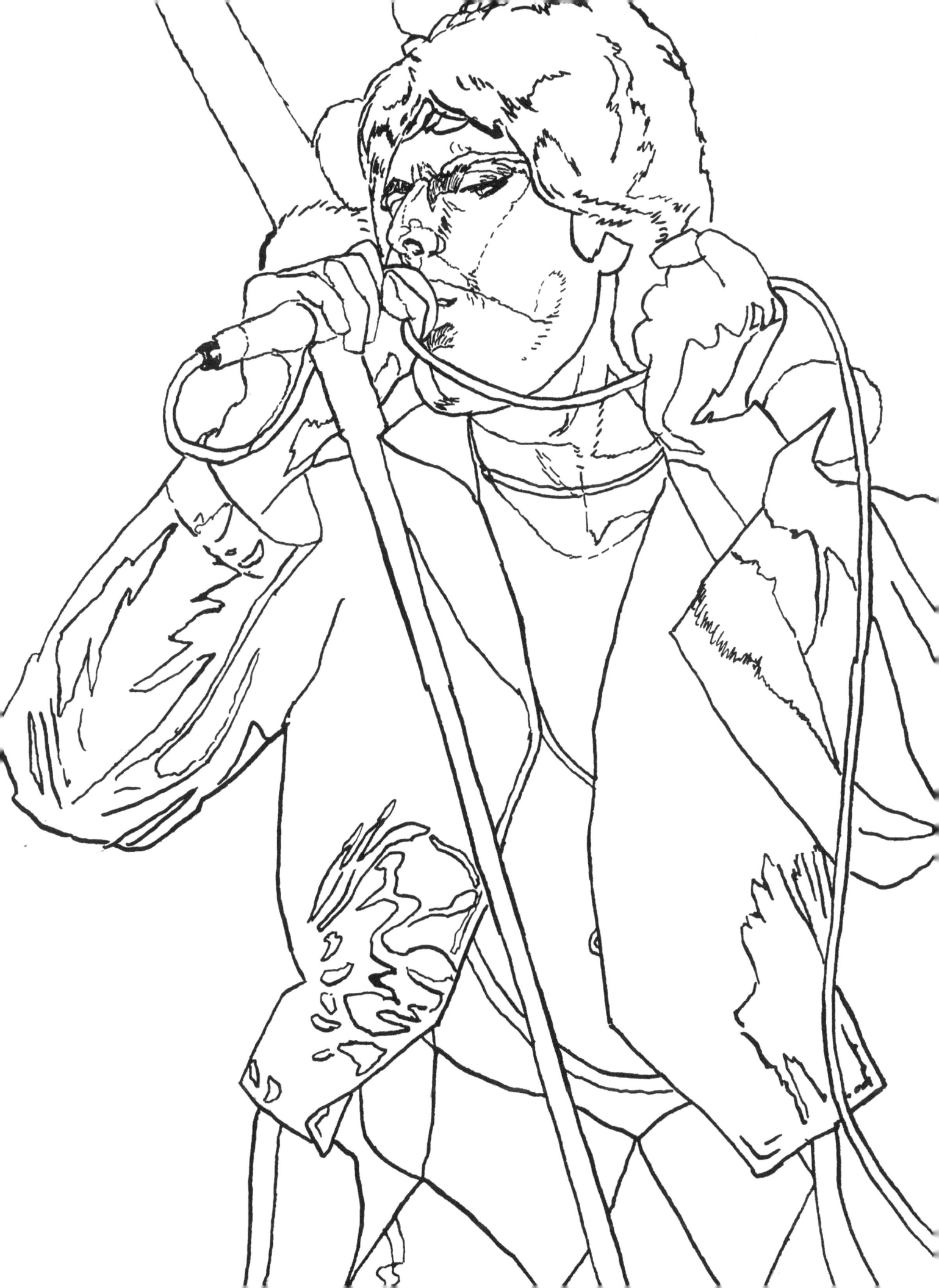

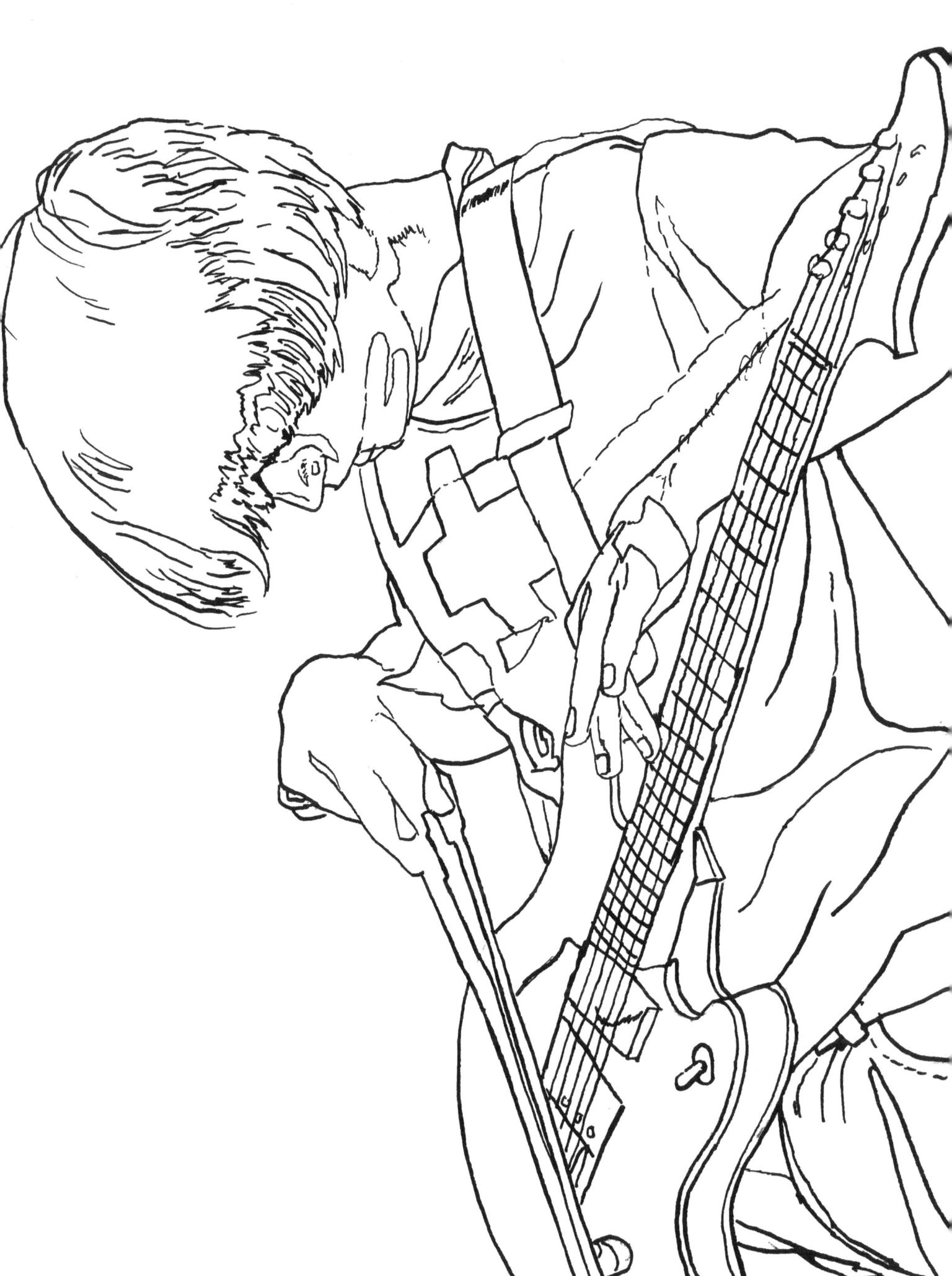

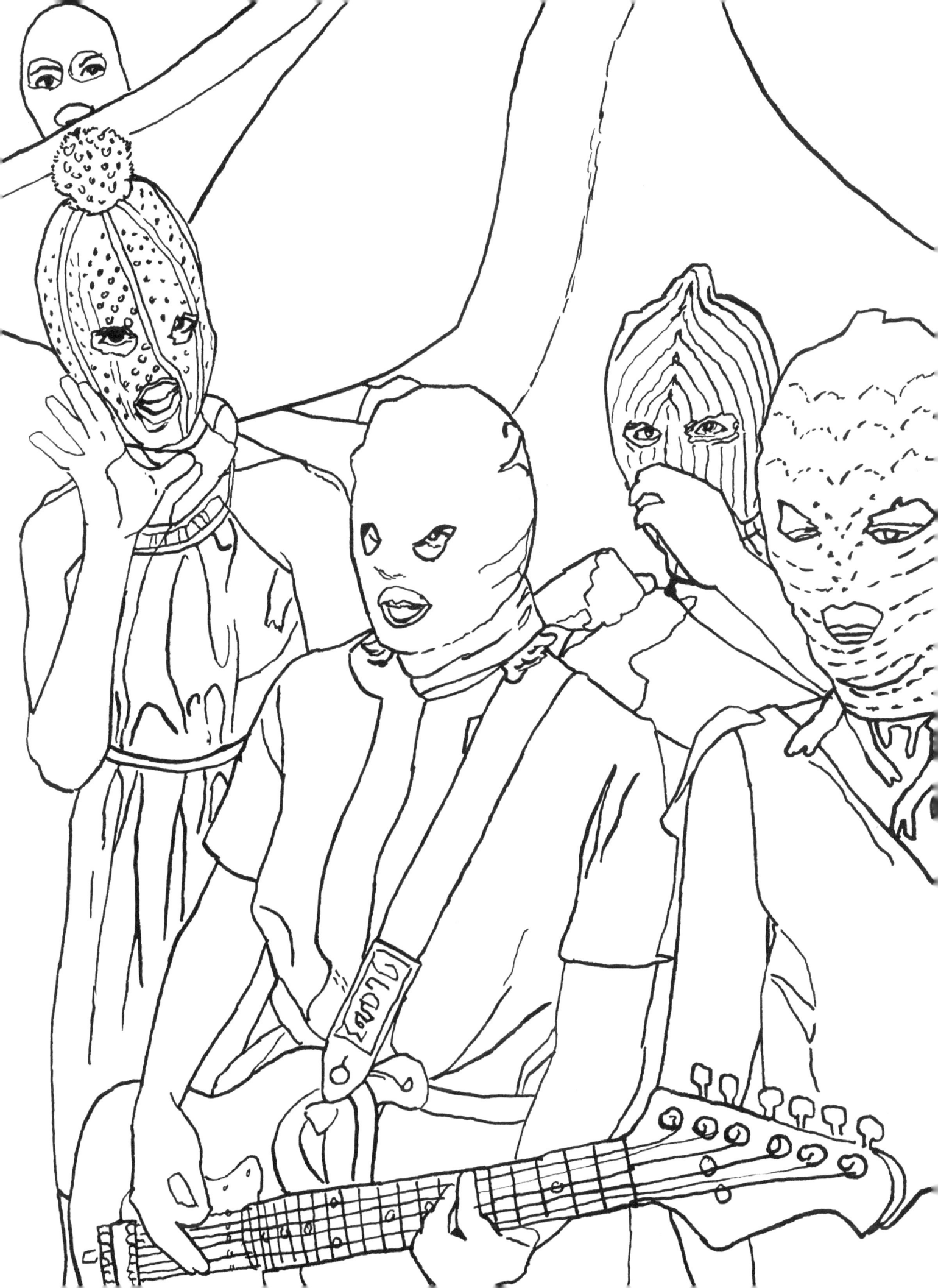

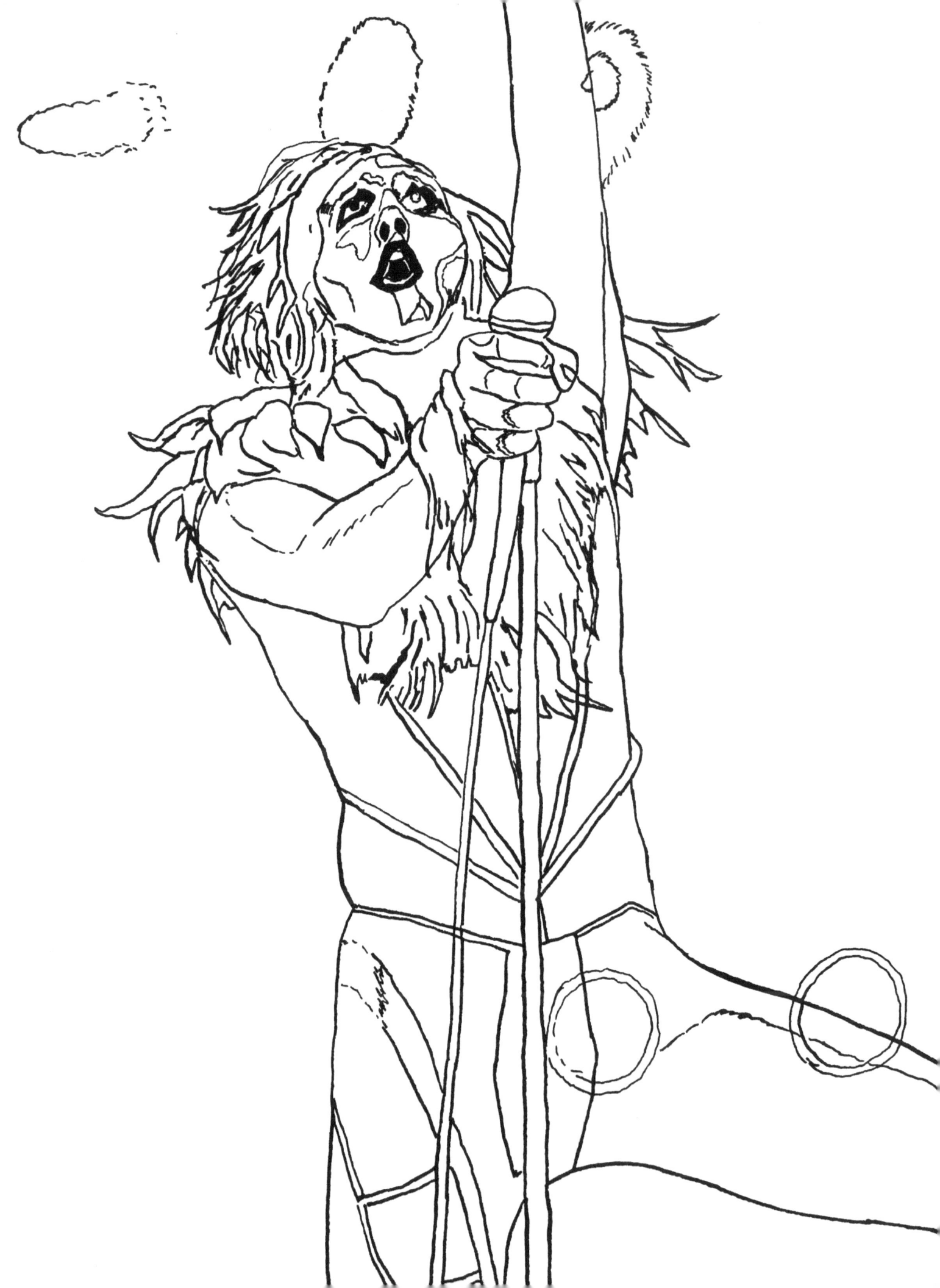

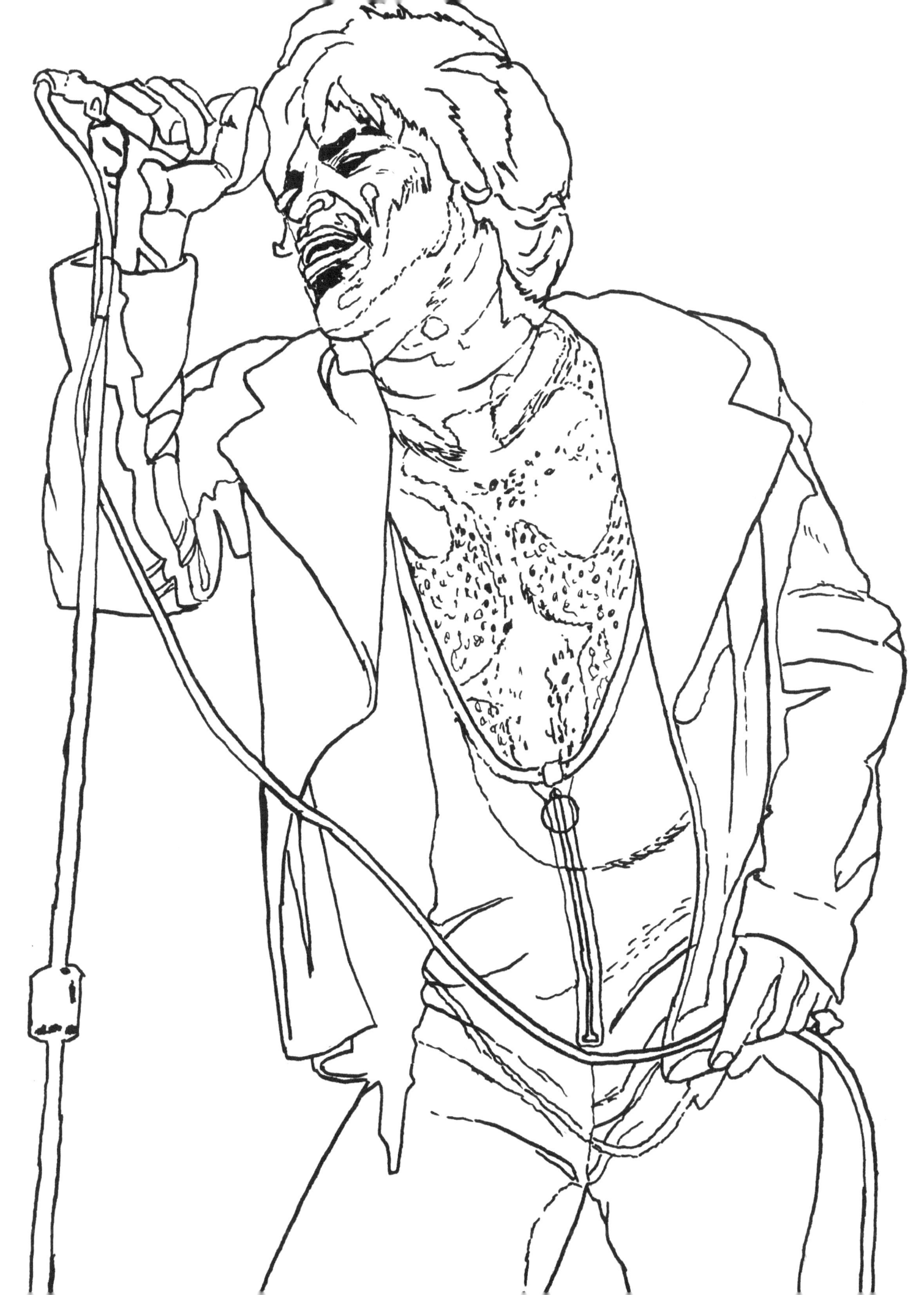

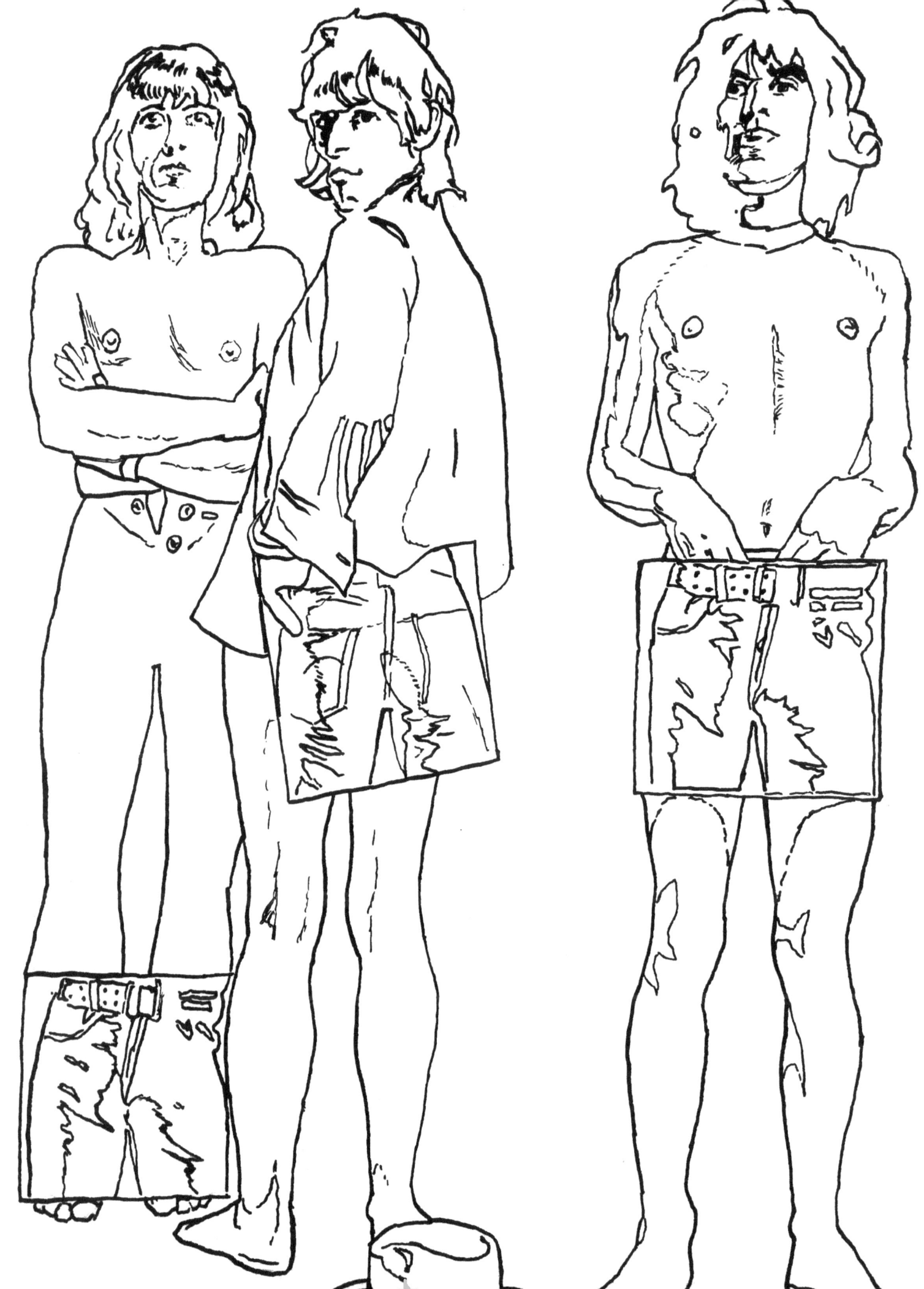

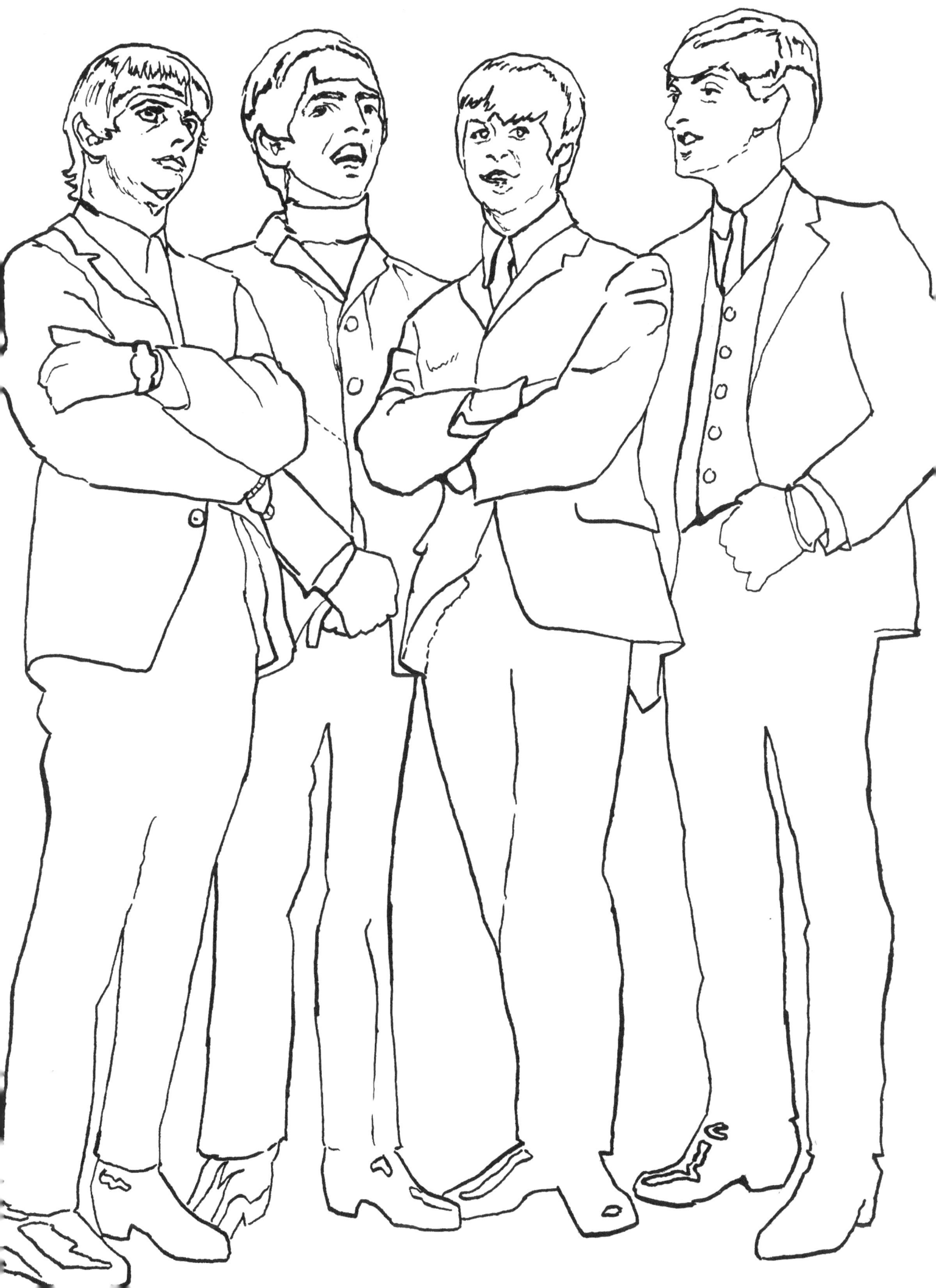

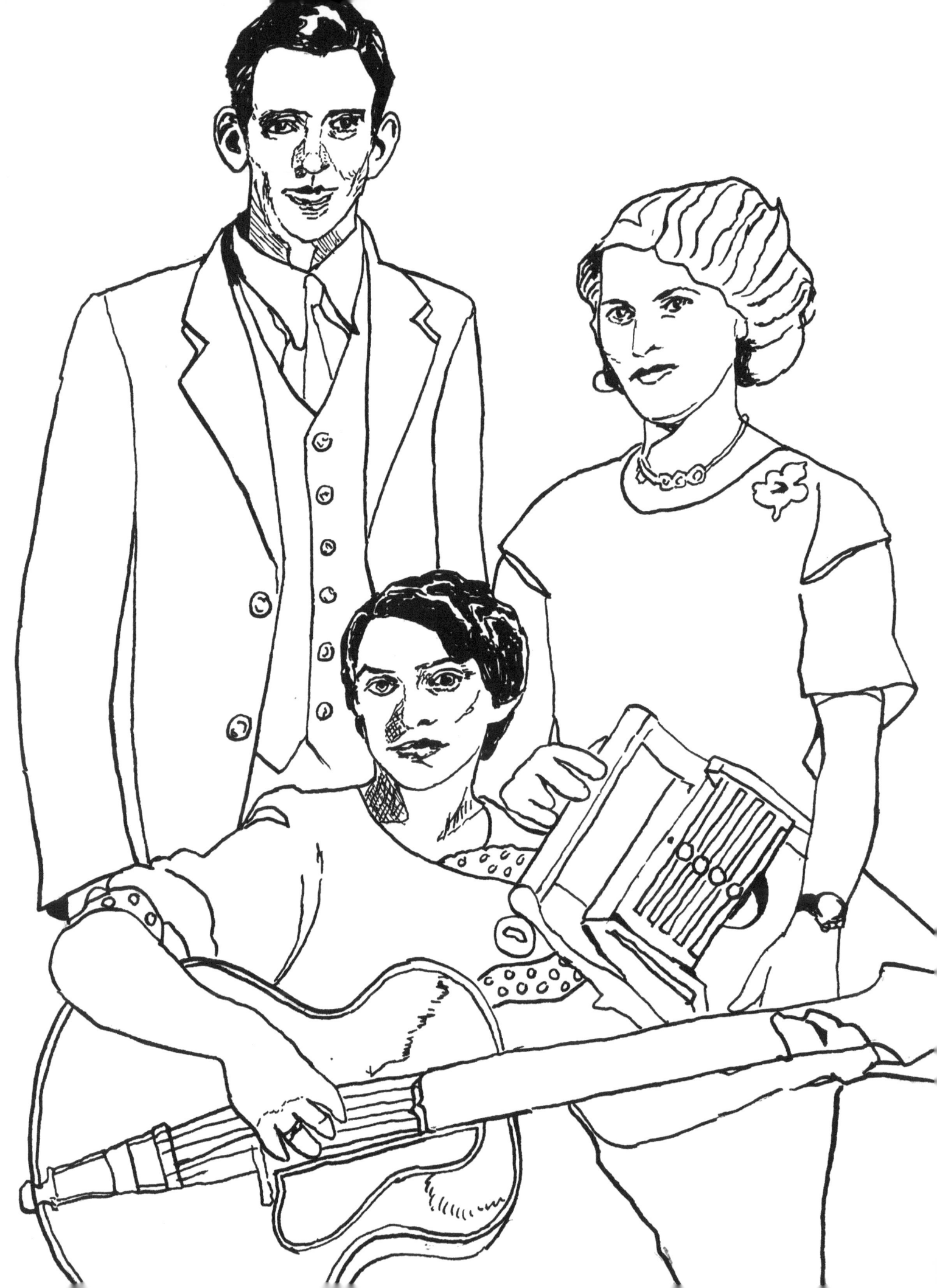

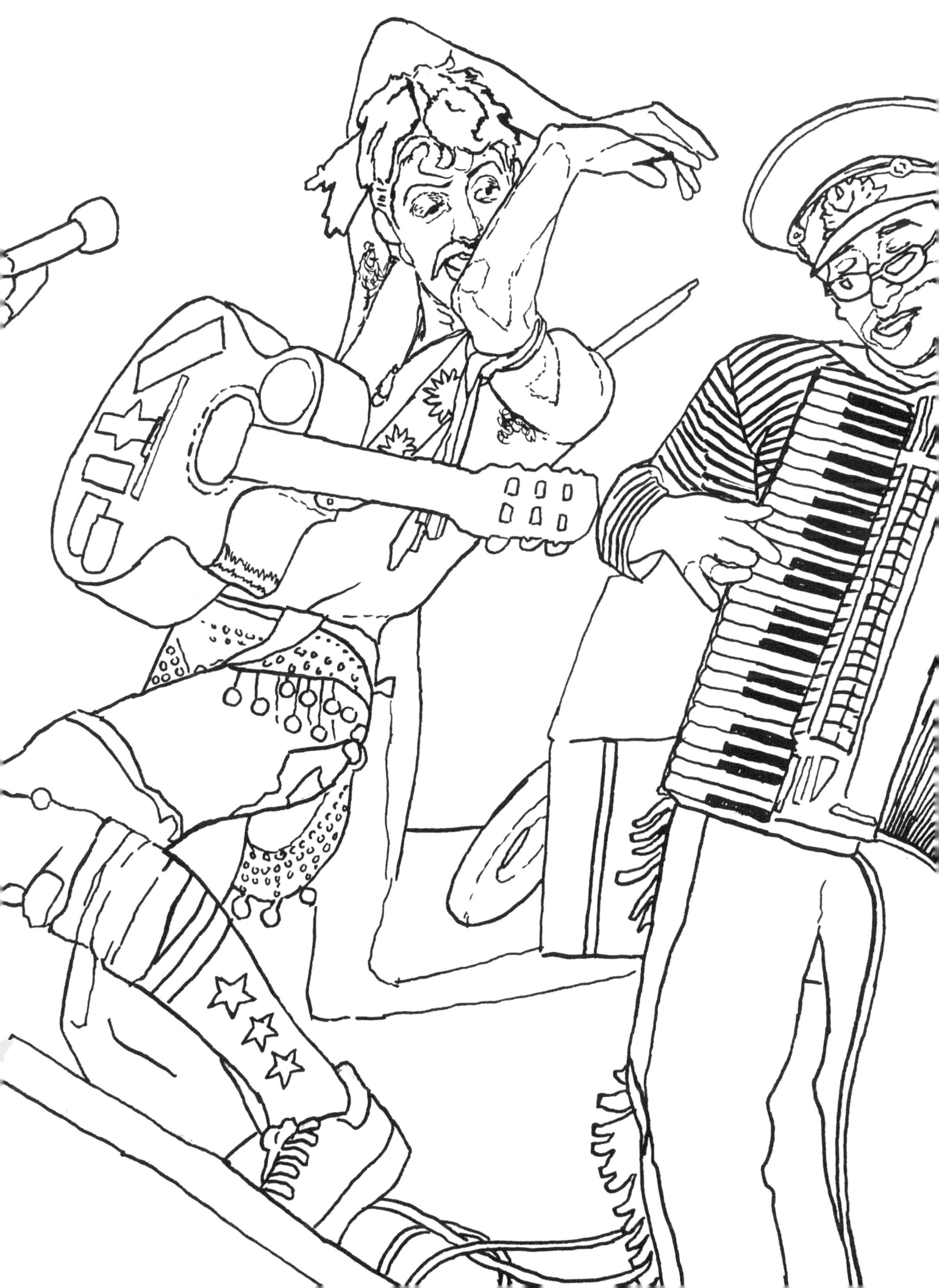

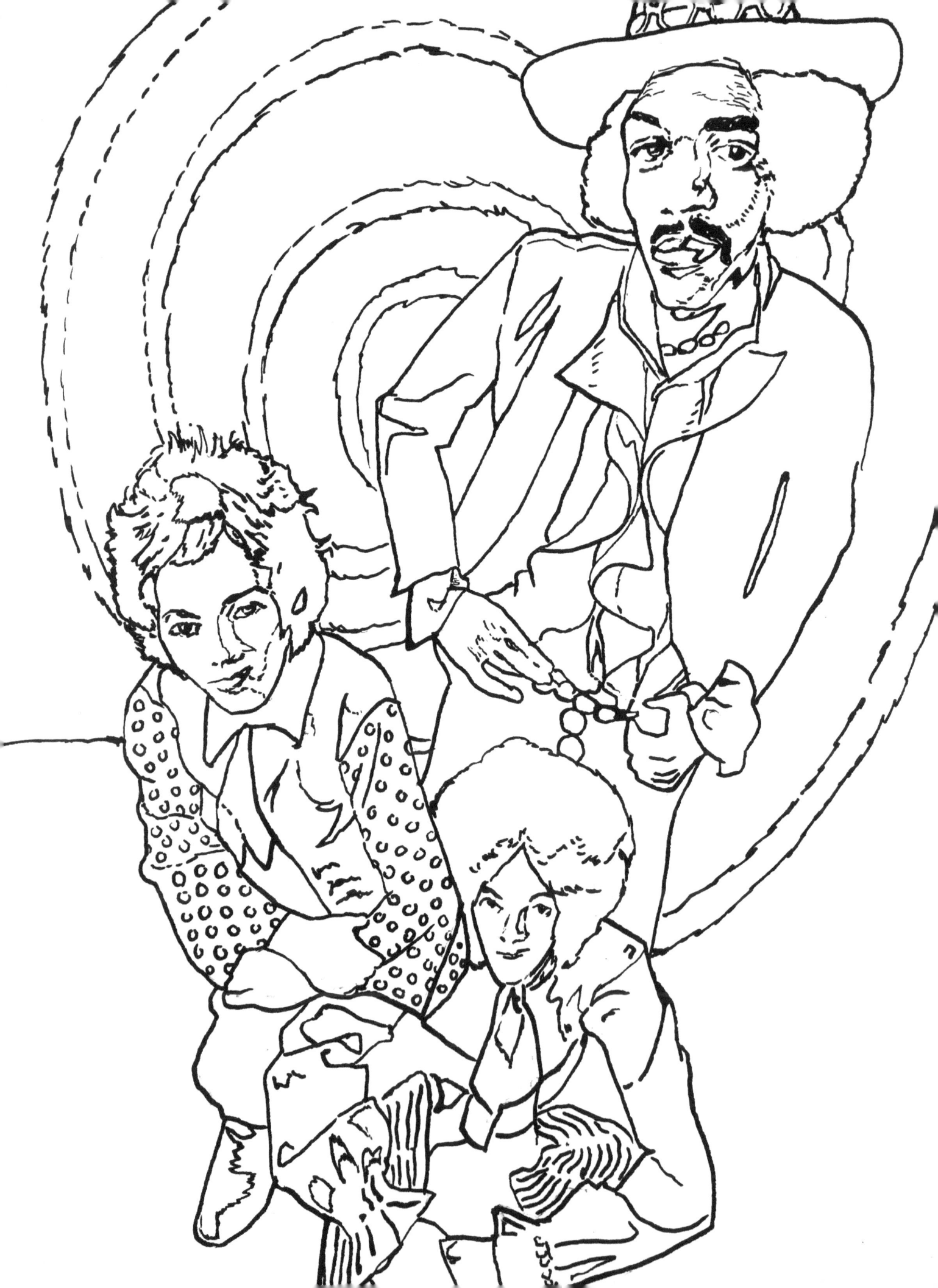

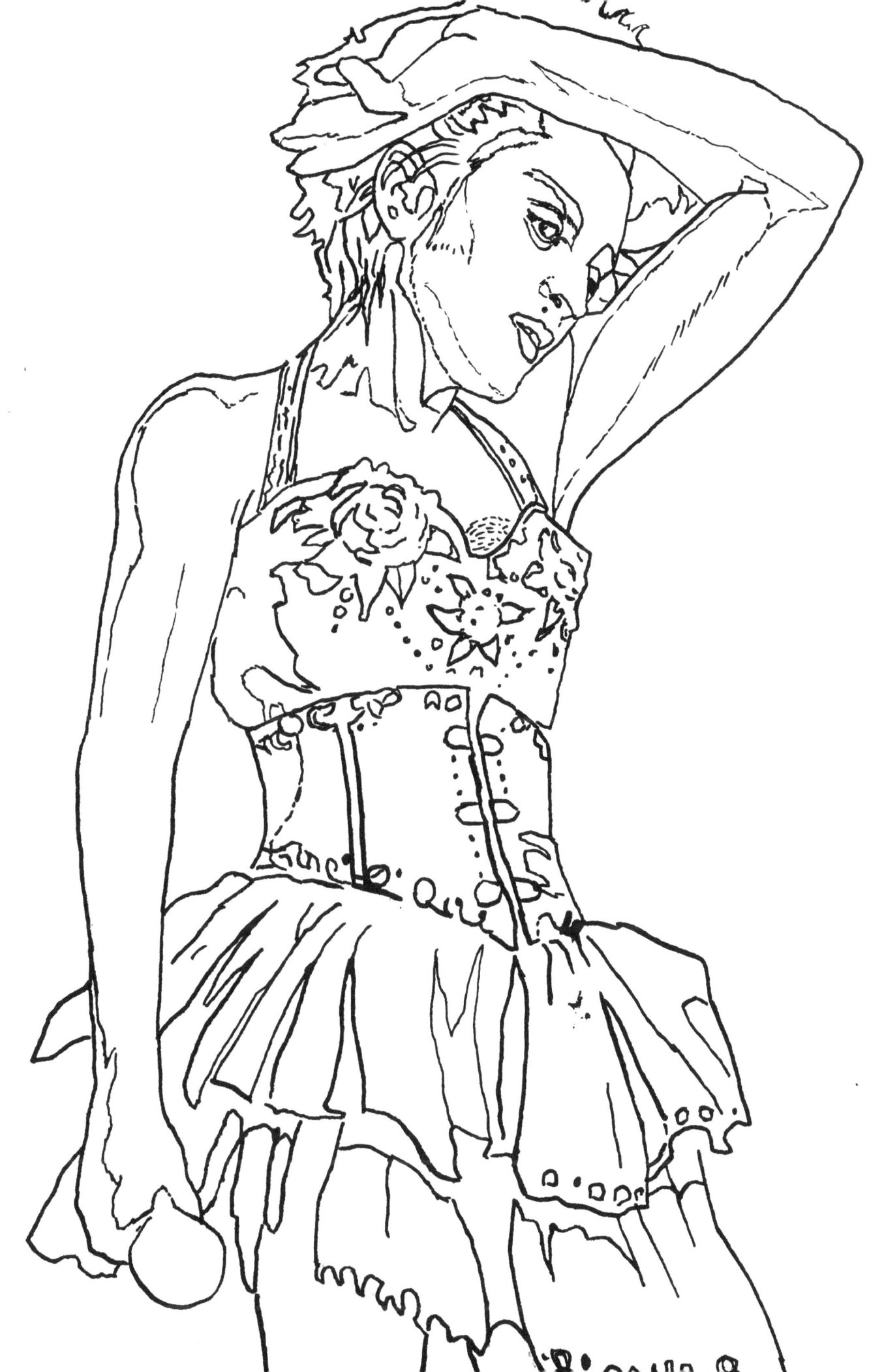

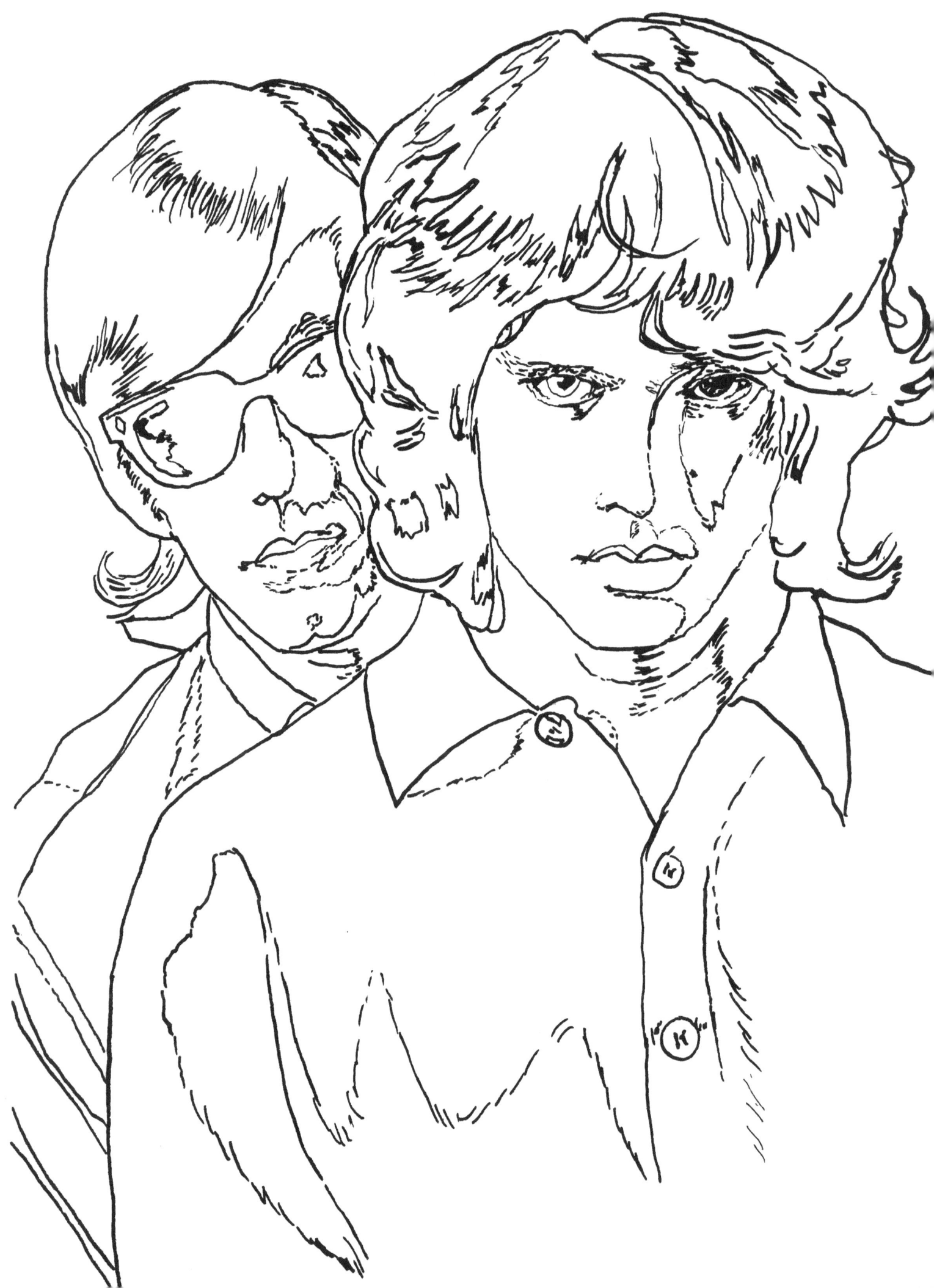